The social history of Canada

MICHAEL BLISS, EDITOR

THE UNSOLVED RIDDLE OF SOCIAL JUSTICE

AND OTHER ESSAYS

The social criticism of Stephen Leacock

EDITED AND INTRODUCED BY ALAN BOWKER

UNIVERSITY OF TORONTO PRESS

© University of Toronto Press 1973
Toronto and Buffalo
Printed in Canada
ISBN (casebound) 0-8020-1997-8
ISBN (paperback) 0-8020-6201-6
LC 73-79860

Dates of original publication

'Greater Canada: An Appeal' 1907
'Literature and Education in America' 1909
'The Apology of a Professor: An Essay on Modern Learning' 1910
'The Devil and the Deep Sea: A Discussion of Modern Morality' 1910
'The Woman Question' 1915
'The Tyranny of Prohibition' 1919
The Unsolved Riddle of Social Justice 1920

Contents

An introduction

BY ALAN BOWKER

'DO NOT ever try to be funny,' Stephen Leacock once told a young friend, 'it is a terrible curse. Here is a world going to pieces and I am worried. Yet when I stand up before an audience to deliver my serious thoughts they begin laughing. I have been advertised to them as funny and they refuse to accept me as anything else.'[1] Such has been Leacock's fate over the years. He is remembered as the best-selling humorist in the English language from 1910 to 1925, the man who made three generations perceive their foibles and forget their troubles, the genial jester whose sunshine humour put Mariposa on the literary map of the world. A grateful public has named mountains and schools and medals after him, has put his smiling comic face on a postage stamp, but has paid only grudging and even apologetic recognition to the fact that he was also a professor of political economy, more than half of whose published writings were of a highly serious nature.

In his later life, Leacock agreed to wear the comic mask his public demanded. Seeking affection and proud of his ability to conjure up laughter, he almost – but never quite – drowned his serious voice in a flood of mirth. The public then and since has been content to ignore Leacock the social scientist altogether. By doing so, we have deprived ourselves of a perceptive Canadian social critic who had much to say about his world – and ours; and we have made him seem a smaller, narrower, and less significant figure in our history than he actually was. This book is an attempt to remedy this distortion by re-examining Leacock's life and thought in the years before 1921, and by presenting to the modern reader some of the best of his early writings on imperialism, education and culture, religion and morality, feminism, prohibition, and social justice.

Stephen Leacock was born in England in 1869, and as a boy of six migrated with his family to a small backwoods farm near Sutton, Ontario. After private tuition, he was educated at Upper Canada College and at the University of Toronto, where he studied 'languages, living, dead, and half-dead,' and then was forced by poverty to enter school-teaching. From 1889 to 1899 he was Modern Language Master at Upper Canada, where, according to Principal (Sir) George Parkin, he 'gained the reputation of being a very excellent teacher.' 'In some ways,' Parkin told Leacock's later employer, Principal Peterson of McGill, 'he was the most clever, ready and versatile man that I had here on the whole staff.'[2]

Upper Canada College must have been in many ways an interesting place for a young master in the 1890s. Parkin was appointed principal in 1895, after having pursued a successful career as speaker and writer in the cause of imperial unity; he brought to the college high ideals, an acquaintance with men and affairs, and a zeal for the British Empire, which inspired masters and boys alike. Under his influence Upper Canada produced a disproportionate number of the leaders of the imperialist movement in the next generation. Leacock's contemporaries as masters there included Pelham Edgar, W.L. Grant, and E.R. Peacock.

But Leacock did not consider himself fortunate. He always hated school-teaching, which he called 'the most dreary, the most thankless, and the worst paid profession in the world.' Parkin noted this dissatisfaction. 'In some ways I do not think him exactly suited for being a school master, and especially a house master, as he was somewhat impatient of the infinite detail and routine necessary in a residential school. I always told him that Professorial work was more completely in his line than housemastership.'[3]

Feeling his considerable talents wasted in the routine of teaching, Leacock sought a way out. Between 1894 and 1898 he wrote a fairly large number of humorous sketches which were published in several Canadian and American magazines. But these brought slight fame and slighter remuneration, and this career was abandoned. A more promising avenue was political economy, which Leacock began to study privately about 1895. In 1899, he left teaching to begin graduate study at the University of Chicago. After a brilliant career there he presented his thesis on 'The Doctrine of Laissez-Faire' and was awarded his PH D. 'The meaning of this degree,' he later wrote, 'is that the recipient of instruction is examined for the last time in his life, and is pronounced completely full. After this, no new ideas can be imparted to him.'

At Chicago, Leacock was exposed to the latest progressive political economy. In the previous thirty years, German-trained American scholars had challenged the precepts of the classical economists and were propounding a far more positive role for the state in regulating monopolies, influencing the economy, and caring for the welfare of the citizen. Social Darwinism, once dominant in economics and sociology, was being repudiated or at least modified to stress man's collective rather than his individual survival. Four teachers in particular made an impression on Leacock: Henry Pratt Judson, Caspar Miller, J. Laurence Laughlin, and especially Thorstein Veblen.[4] Leacock may have read Veblen's *Theory of the Leisure Class* before going to Chicago, and much of his later work bears the stamp of Veblen's ideas. It is worth noting, however, that Veblen did not impress Leacock as a teacher; and his cynicism, detachment, and proposals for technocracy were repugnant to his Canadian pupil.[5] Though Leacock returned to work in his native land and was an ardent imperialist, the influence of the Chicago school shows in all his social science writings and in his preoccupation with American problems in addition to those of Canada and the Empire.

Now fortune began to smile on Leacock. In 1900 he married the grand-daughter of Sir Henry Pellatt, millionaire financier, imperialist, and later builder of Toronto's Casa Loma; the following year he began his thirty-five-year career as teacher of political economy at McGill. 'Personally, he is very taking,'[6] wrote Principal Peterson after their first meeting, and the judgement was echoed in a few years by the students, the faculty, and many of the most influential men of Montreal. Finally occupying a position which challenged his abilities and satisfied his ambitions, Leacock rose so quickly that by 1905 he was being clearly marked out by his principal as the likely successor to the head of his department.[7] In 1906 Leacock capped his meteoric ascent by publishing a textbook, *Elements of Political Science*. It was immediately successful and remained throughout his life Leacock's best-selling book. More than three dozen American universities adopted it, but its greatest influence lay in the British Empire, China, and Japan, where it was used for two generations. The following year he published *Baldwin, Lafontaine, Hincks: Responsible Government* in the 'Makers of Canada' series, and accompanied this with several scholarly and popular papers on the winning of responsible government in Canada. Before 1914 he wrote three volumes in the 'Chronicles of Canada' series, one of which, *The Dawn of Canadian History*, was fairly original in its use of Icelandic sagas and recent scholarship regarding the Norse exploration of America. In a few short years, Leacock had established himself as a writer of considerable range and talent and a scholar of international reputation.

As a young man in a new field of study in a growing country, Leacock had bright prospects for advancement, and ample opportunity for development. Just as he had escaped his personal Slough

of Despond, so Canada itself at the turn of the century shook off a
decade of pessimism and depression and embarked on a wave of
expansion, prosperity, and optimism. 'The poor relation has come
into her fortune,' wrote the British analyst, J.A. Hobson, 'a single
decade has swept away all her diffidence, and has replaced it by a
spirit of boundless confidence and booming enterprise.'[8] Railways
snaked into unpopulated territory, immigrants poured into the 'last,
best west,' miners penetrated the rocky shield, and lumbermen accelerated their assault upon the forest frontier. With the expansion
of industry came urban growth; by 1911 more than half the people
of Ontario and Quebec lived in cities and towns. The boom produced a class of very wealthy men, and it also produced poverty,
slums, urban blight, and alienation. Intellectuals like Leacock, looking at these rapid changes, gave their concerned attention to the new
problems of materialism, urbanism, and an altered social structure.
Moreover, the sense of fulfilled destiny brought by the great boom,
coupled with the consciousness of new responsibilities and new
dangers in a world beginning to lose the peace and security of *pax
Britannica,* produced a heated debate about the relationship between
mother country and colony. It was in this discussion of imperial
relations that Leacock first made his public mark.

In 1905 Governor-General Lord Grey, himself an ardent imperialist, asked Principal Peterson for a promising young lecturer to
conduct a university extension course in the capital city. Peterson
recommended Leacock as a man who could, as Grey put it, 'wake up
Ottawa + keep it awake.'[9] Leacock lived up to every expectation,
dazzling the audience (which included not only the students, but
Grey and his entourage, MP's, cabinet ministers, and senior civil
servants) with a series of brilliant lectures on 'The British Empire,'
which provoked widespread attention and debate.[10] As a result,
Leacock was soon being asked to speak all over eastern Canada. In
May 1906, the cream of Toronto's social élite packed Massey Hall to
hear and cheer him. Early the following year a Montreal audience
gave him a five-minute standing ovation.[11] Within a few months
Leacock had established himself as one of the best platform orators
in the country. In April 1907, he distilled the essence of his imperialist ideas into a piece of perfervid rhetoric called 'Greater Canada: An
Appeal' which he delivered as a speech and published as a pamphlet.
This speech, which provoked considerable controversy, is the first of
the selections reprinted in this volume.

As a popular lecturer Leacock displayed few of the trademarks of his later humorous performances. His eyes were steely blue, flashing more often than twinkling as he approached the climax of a theme. His body was straight and imposing, his great head commanding, his hair and his clothes as neat as was possible for Leacock. His greatest asset was his resonant voice, which moulded his carefully fashioned rhetoric into a powerful engine of persuasion. With all the arts of the actor he manipulated the emotions of his listeners, using now humour, now anger, now biting satire, now soaring idealism, now a boastful swagger, to sweep the audience up in his own imperialist fervour. He never chuckled.[12]

The imperialist governor-general was enthusiastic about his new 'find.' 'He is an excellent lecturer [:] clear [,] crisp [,] condensed [,] comprehensive...' 'He has all Parkin's enthusiasm for the Empire,' he told Peterson, 'and in style, matter, and general effectiveness he is Parkin's superior.' In 1907 Grey decided on 'turning Dr Leacock loose ... as an Imperial missionary,'[13] and enlisted the aid of influential friends in England and Canada to secure contacts and audiences for Leacock around the Empire. His aim was to find an apostle of imperialism to replace the aging Parkin, who had made a similar tour twenty years earlier. Evidently he hoped that, inspired by his memorable experience, dazzled by his contact with those in high places, and full of information and a sense of mission, Leacock would devote his life to the imperialist cause as Parkin had.

With the exception of one incident, the tour was a personal triumph for Leacock. Glowing reports reached Grey and Peterson from all over the Empire testifying to the conspicuous success of their missionary. Leacock also fulfilled his other duty, of making contacts. 'I saw a great many people in London,' he wrote at the start of his tour; 'went to lunch with Mr Balfour, stayed in the country with Rudyard Kipling and saw a good deal of Jebb,[14] Fabian Ware (Editor, Morning Post) and Amery of the Times.'[15] Elsewhere in the Empire he had access to some of the political and intellectual leaders of the various Dominions, such as Smuts of South Africa, Prime Minister Deakin of New Zealand, and high officials of the Indian civil service. His tour, which lasted from April 1907 to March 1908, took him through eastern Canada, England, Australia, New Zealand, South Africa, and the Canadian west.

There were, however, certain aspects of Leacock's imperialist performances which disquieted those who had hoped to use him.

Imperial preaching was delicate business, fraught with the threat of offending sensibilities and touching off political explosions. Leacock was not the man to restrain his ebullience or to follow anyone else's 'line.' Grey's criticism of Leacock's Ottawa lectures was that they were too anti-American. 'It is quite possible to crow + flap one's wings without treading on one's neighbour's corns,'[16] he wrote. From the British point of view, which Grey represented, even imperial sentiment and Canadian nationalism could not be allowed to interfere with the cardinal principle of British policy, the achievement of rapport with the United States. Leacock made a much more serious blunder on his arrival in England in May 1907, by contributing an article to the *Morning Post* which deplored the failure of the Imperial Conference to take the steps toward Imperial unity which he had advocated in 'Greater Canada.' The article, 'John Bull, Farmer,' was an allegory in American dialect comparing the colonies to the sons of a farmer too set in the old ways to realize the benefits of a family partnership. It concluded with this piece of colonial arrogance:

The old man's got old and he don't know it; can't kick him off the place; but I reckon that the next time we come together to talk things over the boys have got to step right in and manage the whole farm.[17]

This satire touched off a 'rumpus' which swept through the British and Canadian press and brought a good deal of editorial censure on Leacock's head. Winston Churchill called it 'offensive twaddle.'[18] Peterson tactfully told Leacock that 'your friends here feel that you have gone quite far enough on that tack.' Later he summarized the indictment: 'much of your offense consisted in rushing in where, by tacit compact, the genuine Canadian is afraid to tread.'[19]

This feeling on the part of officials sensitive to political hazards, that Leacock was a man who might do more harm than good, may be one reason why he never achieved the career as imperial missionary which had seemed to be marked out for him. In 1913, in response to a suggestion from Lionel Curtis that Leacock write an article for the *Round Table* on the naval situation, George Wrong doubtless expressed the prevailing feeling among 'establishment' imperialists when he replied that he did not think this would be 'quite safe.'[20] In any case, a man of Leacock's talents and ambitions probably had too many other interests to devote his life to a single cause. Indeed, he seems to have tired quickly enough of the hurly-burly world of proselytizing and politics, and longed to get away from it all; during the two summers following his return he gave up lucrative speaking tours to build his summer home on Old Brewery Bay near Orillia. Thus his withdrawal was largely voluntary. He never lost his zeal for the Empire, and continued to contribute brilliant articles on imperialism to English and Canadian magazines. He was a member of the Montreal Round Table group, though he was never very active and the group itself was usually moribund.

Only once before the war did Leacock throw himself into a political cause with the ardour he had shown for imperialism. In the 1911 election he campaigned actively against the proposed reciprocity agreement with the United States. He wrote full-page articles for newspapers across the country, for which he was paid by the Canadian Home Market Association, a front-group of the Canadian Manufacturers Association (which also paid for their distribution through a press service).[21] He made a speaking tour through Quebec and the Maritimes, and he played a major role in the campaigns in Orillia and in Brome, where he helped a political unknown defeat a cabinet minister. He was exultant at the outcome, which he considered as 'a plebiscite of the eight million people of this half of the continent in expression of their earnest wish for an enduring union with the Empire.'[22]

After 1908 Leacock increasingly turned his attention to the writing of serious but informal essays on social problems. He derived much of his inspiration from his close friend (Sir) Andrew Macphail, who took over the *University Magazine* in 1907 and made it the most influential Canadian periodical of its day. Leacock helped in the editing of it (especially after Macphail went overseas during the war) and was a major contributor. Besides articles on imperialism, he produced in 1909 and 1910 a series of three balanced essays which fitted together and may have been intended as part of a larger cycle representing Leacock's views on life and social questions. These essays, 'Literature and Education in America,' 'The Apology of a Professor,' and 'The Devil and the Deep Sea,' are reprinted in this volume. If Leacock intended to write further essays along these lines, he never completed the task, though he later added one essay similar in theme and tone, 'The Woman Question' (1915), which is also reprinted here.

Any plans Leacock may have had for a career as an essayist were shattered by a fortuitous occurrence which changed the course of his life. In 1910 he gathered the humorous sketches he had written at Upper Canada, added some new ones, and published *Literary Lapses.* To his astonishment he suddenly found himself a best-selling humorist with a public clamouring for more. To satisfy this demand Leacock began to pour forth a stream of sketches, satires, and articles, which at the end of each year he would put into a book to catch the Christmas trade. Eventually his success as a humorist destroyed his effectiveness as a social scientist; for not even Leacock could hope to follow successfully two careers, either of which would have taxed the strength of an ordinary man. But the depletion of his academic resources did not become fully apparent until the 1920s. Initially Leacock's effectiveness as a political economist and social commentator was actually enhanced by his emergence as a humorist. Not only did he now have a wide audience, which devoured his every book, serious and silly, but he had found a new vehicle for his social ideas which was far more economical, inclusive, and persuasive than the relatively diffuse informal essay. By fusing humour with the insights of the social scientist, Leacock produced his finest achievements in either field, *Sunshine Sketches of a Little Town* (1912), and *Arcadian Adventures with the Idle Rich* (1914).

The publication of *Arcadian Adventures* coincided with the outbreak of the First World War. For years Leacock had warned of the German menace, denouncing the German Empire as the home of autocracy and decadent aristocracy, not to mention most of the academic trends he detested. 'This,' he announced, 'is the war of the free peoples against the peoples still in chains. ... Who that believes in humanity or God, can doubt the end?'[23] Leacock plunged eagerly into the war effort, supporting the militia movement at McGill, speaking at patriotic meetings and recruiting rallies, and producing articles and pamphlets such as *National Organization for War* (1917), which was distributed by the Canadian government and attracted favourable notice in England. His humour was put into war service as well; in sketch after sketch he lampooned Germany, attacked profiteers and shirkers, and extolled thrift, sacrifice, and patriotism. In 1916 he gave his first extended humorous lecture tour for the

Belgian Relief Fund. He also entered a number of the debates which the war engendered. He favoured conscription, but opposed all coercion of Quebec and defended the French Canadians from charges of slacking and disloyalty. He opposed female suffrage, criticized the manner of enacting the income tax, and attacked government ownership of railways as economically disastrous.[24]

With the end of the Great War, Leacock, like most thinking Canadians, turned with trepidation to the problems of peace. One issue in particular that caught his attention was the movement for prohibition which in 1919 and 1920 swept across North America, engulfing – or drying up – all opposition. Its proponents saw it as a triumph for the sentiments of moral uplift and spiritual regeneration brought to fever pitch by the war. Leacock denounced it as the work of a 'relentless and fanatical minority' which had donned the 'false mantle of religion and morality' to perpetrate 'the most un-British agitation that has come to us in half a century.' As one of the very few who dared to speak openly against the crusade, Leacock made it clear that he would lecture anywhere, any time, without fee, to any group combatting prohibition laws. His efforts stung the prohibitionists sufficiently that by 1921 some of them raised a clamour to have him removed from McGill.[25] He expressed his viewpoint most strongly in 'The Tyranny of Prohibition' (1919), which was published in Britain and the United States.

The prohibition struggle was only a small part of the social crisis facing Canada and North America in 1919. The war had produced in all classes what Leacock called 'National Hysteria,' the sort of crusading idealism and intolerance of opposition which animated the prohibitionists. While Leacock valued the wartime spirit of national solidarity and individual self-sacrifice, he realized also that such passions, out of control or misled by ignorant utopians or inept and selfish politicians, could produce social catastrophe. All the problems of the great boom, which for two decades had strained the fabric of Canadian society, were exacerbated by the war, and suddenly and peremptorily demanded solution. Business and labour were at daggers drawn. The drift of people from farms to cities accelerated, as did the growth of urban slums. Regionalism, racial conflict, and economic recession mocked the confidence of the young Dominion in its destiny. Each class or group in society – women, returned soldiers, labourers, farmers, socialists, temperance men, religious revivalists, businessmen, scientists, intellectuals, and politicians, – came forward with a blueprint for Utopia which it pressed noisily, dogmatically, and sometimes violently. Over the babble of discordant voices hung a black cloud of Bolshevism, which by mid-year was winning its civil war in Russia, had toppled governments in Hungary, Germany, and Bavaria, and was threatening elsewhere in Europe. The extent of this social passion and social bitterness was shown by the appalling suddenness with which the Winnipeg General Strike, in common with similar strikes in Seattle and Boston, broke down into class conflict and violence. It seemed to a jittery intelligentsia and panic-stricken governments to be a portent of the social chaos which threatened all North America. Daily reports by a sensational press of strikes, lockouts, riots, bombings, parades, lynchings, raids, and trials in the United States added fuel to these fears.

'Never...' wrote Leacock, 'was there a moment in which there was greater need for sane and serious thought.' (See page 75, *infra.*) In answer to this need Leacock wrote a series of articles for the New York *Times* in the fall of 1919, which he published in book form early the following year as *The Unsolved Riddle of Social Justice.* In it he tried to explain as simply as possible, to the largest audience he could reach, what had caused the present difficulties and what solutions were possible. To make the book widely relevant, Leacock refrained from references to specific places or incidents, and spoke only of those social problems which he took to be common to all industrial societies. Further, he published the book in a format designed to match that of his humorous publications and had it distributed with all the fanfare of a funny book. The jibes of his fellow academics were predictable, the reviews were mixed, but Leacock had done what he had set out to do. No one who reads *The Unsolved Riddle,* however he may react to its overblown and rhetorical style, or whatever his opinion of the solutions (or lack thereof) which Leacock offers, can fail to be impressed by the range of material covered, the persuasiveness of the argument, and the utter sincerity of tone which runs through the work. This was not a piece of hackwork for Leacock but a vitally important task which he performed to the best of his ability, and of which he was proud.

The publication of *The Unsolved Riddle* ended a phase of Leacock's career, though no man's life may ever be neatly cut up into 'periods' or 'phases.' After 1920 he gave his attention increasingly to his career as a humorist, and in 1921 he reached the peak of his fame with his highly successful English tour. Prosperity appeared to restore social harmony, though many of the riddles of social justice remained unsolved. Imperialism was a dead letter, as Leacock had to admit in revising the chapter on 'Imperial Federation' in *Elements* in 1921. A world seeking gaiety and novelty after the harsh experience of war provided an insatiable market for humour, and Leacock strained his talents to supply this demand. The Leacock who is most familiar to the public, the man with the crinkled face and twinkling eyes who made economics 'fun' and laughed away the summer in bucolic splendour at Old Brewery Bay, at last emerged triumphant.

Leacock never entirely abandoned his use of humour as a vehicle for social commentary, but its tone became milder and its note more forced. The great depression and another war revived his crusading spirit and social concern, and he again produced pamphlets, books, articles, and speeches advocating imperial reorganization, national development, currency reform, and social action to solve what was now 'The Riddle of the Depression.' These proposals were in large part repetitious of his pre-1920 programmes, and they were increasingly half-baked and badly written. While his economic theories and anti-socialist diatribes may have seemed comforting and plausible to men such as George Drew, Howard Ferguson, and R.B. Bennett, they became increasingly irrelevant and irritating to some of his younger students such as Eugene Forsey and David Lewis, who had other solutions to the riddle. What the public wanted from Leacock were funny stories and homely wisdom to drive away for a moment the dark clouds of depression and war, and to provide reassurance about the future; they treated his social concern merely as evidence of his goodness of heart, and his theories as the eccentricities of a very funny man. The man who smiled on hearing the news of Leacock's death, because it provided the occasion for reprinting some of his funny sayings, embodied the prevailing spirit of Canadians at the graveside of their most famous *littérateur*. Few, if any, mourned the passing of the social scientist, whose relevance, if not his spirit, had long since expired.

'I ... am an Imperialist because I will not be a Colonial,' Leacock proclaimed in 1907 in 'Greater Canada.' (p. 4) His imperialism was an expression of his pride and confidence in his country's future, but equally it was the product of his fears that the materialism and commercialism brought by the great boom would sap the moral fibre of the new nation. In two ways, then, Canada must become 'something greater or something infinitely less.' (p. 6)

Continuing as a colony would be bad, but independence would be worse. Whatever her future prospects, Canada faced external threats in the present which she was simply too weak to counter. The United States, Leacock believed, had always harboured aggressive designs on Canada, and he regarded the Monroe Doctrine not as a protection against European foes, but as a blueprint for continental hegemony. Like many imperialists, he viewed the United States as a land sunk in materialism and corruption. He knew that an independent Canada would be irresistibly sucked into this vortex by overwhelming American political and economic power. Though Leacock hoped that some day the United States would have a change of heart and rejoin the Empire, he would not tolerate annexation in any form. Canadian independence would only mean the exchange of colonial status for a lower form of subservience.

Even more threatening was the emergence of Germany and Japan as naval powers. Japan was temporarily neutralized by the Anglo-Japanese Treaty, but Leacock believed that she still cast covetous eyes on Canada's Pacific coast. Germany's naval programme threatened the very lifelines of the Empire, and Leacock insisted that it was the duty of the colonies to contribute ships and men if possible, money if necessary, to a united imperial fleet. He was furious in 1913 when the Liberal-dominated Senate killed the Conservative Naval Bill which would have provided the money to build three dreadnoughts as an emergency contribution to the British navy.

Moreover an independent Canada would be destroyed from within by racial and religious strife. Baldwin and Lafontaine, he argued, had shown English and French Canadians how to work in mutual tolerance and forbearance, and Leacock was always careful to acknowledge that the French Canadians were a founding race with equal rights in Canada. Nevertheless, he noted that 'except perhaps for a little bilingual chirruping of an artificial kind in the drawing-rooms of Ottawa and Montreal,'[26] the two races remained divided and racial and religious prejudices ran deep in both. Membership in the Empire would give Canadians a broader patriotism and a nobler mission which could unite the energies of the two peoples, while independence would only focus their jealous attention on local problems.

What Canada had to do, then, was to take the lead in reorganizing the Empire into a federation of equal states under the leadership of the first among equals, Great Britain, with a common fleet, some sort of tariff union, and some kind of federal parliament in which all would be represented. Thus united, Leacock thought, the Anglo-Saxon peoples could get on with their mission of civilizing the backward races and maintaining the peace of the world, by force if necessary. Like most of the imperialists of his generation, Leacock was fond of boasting of the size and heterogeneity of the Empire, which was unlike anything the world had ever seen. It could stand as an object lesson in what good government, justice, and strength in the hands of right, *imperium et libertas,* could achieve. As a branch of the Anglo-Saxon race, Canadians had the opportunity to participate in this noble enterprise; but they would seriously weaken the Empire's chances of performing it if they sulked silent in their tents.

There was, however, a very ugly side to this sense of mission, a haunting fear of the coloured races which burst forth from time to time in Leacock's oratory. In a speech in 1908 he described world history as 'the question of the Aryan civilization of the West and the uncivilized, or at best semi-civilized, people of the Orient. ... There has never been peace and harmony between them.'[27] The British Empire, including Canada, was the front line of the white race in this battle against Asiatic encroachment. Leacock denied that the coloured peoples of the Empire had the same rights as whites. The federation he preached was that of the white Dominions; he always opposed independence or Dominion status for India. In a 1910 article in the *American Political Science Review* he noted approvingly the intention of the South African white, if the native were to revolt, to 'shoot him into marmalade with machine guns.'[28] Like the rest of him, Leacock's racial intolerance and prejudices were larger than life.

Beyond the protection and the mission it offered, imperialism's greatest virtue in Leacock's view was the salutary effect wider horizons and enhanced patriotism would have on Canadian culture and society in the midst of the great boom. As a young people in a new land, Canadians worshipped growth, size, and mastery of nature.

Leacock told a British audience in 1909 that '...if you would see the imaginative side of the Canadian talk with him of railways in the wilderness, of a grain flotilla on the Hudson's Bay and the valley of the Peace broken under the ploughshare. The attraction of the great unknown hinterland that called to it the *voyageurs* and the *coureurs des bois* still holds the soul of the Canadian people.'[29] Leacock shared this fascination; all his life he was full of plans to develop the country, but always feared that great projects would lead to greater pork barrels. The feeling was abroad among Canadians that this was the time to grab a place in society before it was too late. 'We are still as a nation in the groping stage, groping for money,' he wrote in 1911; 'when we have got it, plenty of it, and enough of it, we may hope to turn honest men.'[30] Canadian governments were too often the agencies by which contracts and patronage were distributed, the great hinterland too often a thing to be mined for a quick profit. The west was thrown wide open to 'mere herds of the proletariat of Europe,' and resources and property were lavishly given to speculators and entrepreneurs. 'The development of the interior that should be planned with the majesty, certainty, and symmetry of the building of a Grecian temple, is conducted with the same eager haste as the erection of a circus tent.'[31]

Absorbed in this great quest for wealth and development, localities fought for their share of government spending. Public works became 'words to conjure with,' for they brought growth and development, or at least the appearance thereof. Possession of public office brought control of expending departments whose benefits 'fall upon the constituencies in a fructifying shower';[32] by shrewd spending, governments could entrench themselves in power almost forever, for people were not interested in political issues, but only in getting their share of the loot. Laurier's vaunted policy of national unity was thus to take people's minds off racial and religious questions by focussing their attention on material development, roasting whole the ox of the country's resources, and hoping that people would be eating too greedily to quarrel with each other or to notice that someone else was getting more. Canada was in danger of gaining a whole world but losing her own soul.

This materialist and localist spirit, Leacock cried, must be purged 'in the pure fire of an Imperial patriotism, that is no theory but a passion. This is our need, our supreme need of the Empire – not for its ships and guns, but for the greatness of it, the soul of it, aye for the very danger of it.' ('Greater Canada: An Appeal,' p. 8) Membership in the united Empire would make a 'greater Canada,' not only by fusing her in a larger unit with greater influence, but in the sense that it would liberate the true greatness of the Canadian people from the deadly grip of materialism.

But though he saw a United Empire as the cure for his country's ills, Leacock was never very clear about how it would come into being, or what form it should take. Baldwin and Lafontaine had shown that self-government and nationhood could be consistent with membership in an Empire; now, Leacock felt, it was time to take the next step of establishing some sort of federal council. He hoped that imperial conferences or naval co-operation might be the first step; but his vagueness on these points made him vulnerable. 'Professor Leacock,' wrote the anti-imperialist John S. Ewart, '...ought to have some conception of what it is he is preaching about – some notion, vague or otherwise, of what it is he wants us to do.'[33] What *did* Professor Leacock want us to do? In the final analysis, his imperialism was not a political programme, but a spiritual crusade, designed to create in Canadians that sense of mission and imperial patriotism which would be 'no theory but a passion,' which would save Canadian society from its profound malaise.

The bulk of Leacock's prewar writings expressed his intense antipathy to the materialism and hunger for wealth which seemed to pervade all Canadian society, and which he attacked in his imperialist pronouncements. He could not refrain from expressing in essays and satires his disgust at 'the obvious and glaring fact of the money power, the shameless luxury of the rich, the crude, uncultivated and boorish mob of vulgar men and over-dressed women that masqueraded as high society.'[34] What he said of his friend Macphail he might have said of himself: '...though frequenting the rich in his daily walk of life, [he] was never quite satisfied of their right to be.'[35]

Leacock was too much the political economist, however, to expend all his energy in mere bad-tempered castigation of the rich. He knew that they were only the product of an ideology which permeated all society, rich and poor, and of a series of technological changes which dated from the industrial revolution. This ideology he variously called 'individualism,' 'materialism,' and the 'commercial spirit'; and at different times these terms could mean slightly different things. In general, however, he used these words to refer to something which is an amalgam of three concepts: individualism (or the right of the individual to be an independent and autonomous economic unit), materialism (the defining of things and people by their economic utility), and mastery of nature. After George Grant,[36] we may call these things the animating ideology of the age of progress.

The rise of this ideology and the changes wrought by industrialism are best described in the opening chapters of *The Unsolved Riddle*. The beginnings of the machine age, said Leacock, brought a change in the life of man which separated our age from all that had gone before. Science and the factory system not only reorganized production, but they brought mastery of nature. 'No wonder,' he continued,

that the first aspect of the age of machinery was one of triumph. Man had vanquished nature. The elemental forces of wind and fire, of rushing water and driving storm before which the savage had cowered low for shelter, these had become his servants. The forest that had blocked his path became his field. The desert blossomed as his garden. [p. 78]

Man now saw himself not as a part of nature, but as separate from it, with the right and the power to reshape it to whatever use he thought fit. This idea of mastery, Leacock noted in 'Literature and Education in America' (1909), reached its apogee in North America, and was likely to be equated with progress:

The aspect of primeval nature does not call to our minds the vision of Unseen Powers riding upon the midnight blast. To us the midnight blast represents an enormous quantity of horse-power going to waste; the primeval forest is a first-class site for a saw mill, and the leaping cataract tempts us to erect a red-brick hydro-electric establishment on its banks and make it leap to some purpose. [p. 16]

The industrial revolution broke the old social system. Aristocracy fell to democracy, and the individual was set free to pursue wealth,

self-interest, and mastery of nature. In order to provide the free flow
of capital and labour required to make the factory system function,
the new science of political economy advocated the dissolution of all
institutions and social, legal, or customary restrictions which might
have stood in the way of this freedom. Not only navigation acts and
the like, but all religious restrictions, social inhibitions, or philosophical considerations which in any way impeded the free play of
enlightened self-interest or mastery of nature had to go. Political
economy argued that man was a selfish creature who looked after his
own interests, the economic world ran according to certain natural
laws; *ergo,* by letting men practise self-interest, the state would allow
those natural laws to come into play and so regulate the production,
distribution, and exchange of commodities that supply would tend
to equal demand, the just price for everything would be established,
each man would get what his labour was worth, and social justice
would reign. Social Darwinism put its stamp of approval on this
individualism and materialism by declaring that free competition
between human beings was the way to ensure survival of the fittest.
The old social fabric was thus unravelled, man's power over nature
set loose, and all checks on his selfishness and greed were abandoned. For some, this meant a world of wealth and comfort without
restraint. For others, individualism was 'a sordid boon.' The factory
system

herded [the poor] into factories, creating out of each man a poor miserable atom divorced from hereditary ties, with no rights, no duties,
and no place in the world except what his wages contract may confer on him. Every man for himself, and sink or swim, became the
order of the day. It was nicknamed 'industrial freedom.' [p. 54]

However, the political economists' dreams did not come true. In
The Unsolved Riddle Leacock followed Veblen in noting that in
spite of the great total increase in wealth, riches and poverty still
remained, with the rich getting richer and the poor never seeming to
better their lot. Apparently it proved more profitable to manufacture slightly fewer goods than were needed, rather than to supply
the entire demand; for this practice kept the price a little higher than
it would otherwise have been, while on the other hand ensuring
sufficient sales that large profits could be made and competition was

not invited. Given this slight twist, the laws of the economists worked perfectly, but worked to ensure scarcity, not abundance. Having
produced fewer than enough essential commodities, men then turned to producing things which were somewhat less necessary, and not
enough of those, and so on up the pyramid until a very few purely
luxury goods were being made, and not even enough of those. Those
who owned the means of production got very rich, and were able to
display their wealth in conspicuous consumption, while others were
kept permanently on the edge of starvation, with never quite enough
to buy even the necessities of life. This poverty in turn kept wages
down. The whole system was justified by the laws of economics,
which had been expected to produce Utopia and had in fact
spawned a nightmare.

Unfortunately, in breaking down the institutions which stood in
the way of the free play of these 'natural laws,' men had destroyed
the very things which might have saved them or at least rendered
their existence more tolerable. The decline of these institutions
under the onslaught of the age of progress, and the effects of this
decline, formed the subject of Leacock's unfinished essay cycle of
1909 and 1910.

In 'The Devil and the Deep Sea,' Leacock analyzed the breakdown of organized religion. In the Middle Ages, he argued, fear of
the Devil had impelled ignorant men to do good, and society had
functioned. Then science explained away the Devil as a superstition,
and a society seeking freedom brushed aside the old moral dogmas.
New man-centred religions like Social Darwinism imposed no external imperatives, but justified whatever men decided to do in their
own self-interest; and such religions could be changed if they got in
the way. In the end, there was only one thing man could worship in
a materialist and individualist society: success, however achieved. As
the means were often dubious, 'the new morality shows signs of
exalting the old-fashioned Badness in place of the discredited Goodness. ... Force, brute force, is what we now turn to as the moral
ideal, and Mastery and Success are the sole tests of excellence.' (p.
49) This was bad enough, but now men were reading 'Nitch' and in
their folly deciding that they were supermen. This sort of Faustian
arrogance, Leacock suggested, could only lead to destruction, as man
was a deeply flawed creature who needed external control and

standards of discipline; yet the age of progress had removed all restraints on his selfish passions.

A similar analysis was applied to the decline of learning and philosophy in 'The Apology of a Professor' (1910). Again, the Middle Ages had accepted a certain body of ideas as final truth, and for this truth men would have endured hunger and privation. Then science attacked and disproved these concepts, and materialist and utilitarian values replaced the old dogmatic philosophy. Certitude turned to doubt, as a sceptical and speculative system stressed what man didn't know rather than what he knew. The professor, said Leacock, descended on the social scale from the possessor of priceless truth and wisdom, to a mere 'expert' striving by 'research' to add his contribution to the rubbish-heap of meaningless knowledge; an unlikeable, useless relic knowing only an insignificant part of a minor field. At the same time, continued Leacock, under the pressure of a commercial society the university branched out into new but philosophically and educationally worthless subjects; its organization was bureaucratized, and its 'learning' cut up into 'departments,' 'subjects,' and 'electives.' In the place of the old centre of thought and wisdom was now a mass dispensing agency handing out assorted bits of knowledge to students who faithfully copied and absorbed them in order to get out into their life's work. Soon, Leacock concluded, the professor would vanish altogether and be replaced by the 'Woman with the Spectacles,' 'who ... will dispense the elements of learning cut to order, without an afterthought of what it once has meant.' (p. 39)

It was therefore not surprising that in spite of its mass education, North America in the nineteenth century had produced only a fraction of the literature and general culture that were the glory of Great Britain during the same period. The reason, Leacock concluded in 'Literature and Education in America' (1909), was that where an aristocratic society stressed human excellence, a commercial society stressed 'success':

Social and intellectual values necessarily undergo a peculiar readjustment among a people to whom individually the 'main chance' is necessarily everything. ... Hence all less tangible and provable forms of human merit, and less tangible aspirations of the human mind are rudely shouldered aside by business ability and commercial success. [p. 25]

'The Woman Question' showed how the industrial revolution had destroyed the traditional role of woman as wife, mother, and supervisor of the household. As industrial society crowded people into cities and factories, as the individual became alienated from society, the unity of the family broke down; and women began to demand their 'rights,' i.e. to be considered as economic units to be put to work, produce, and consume, like men. Single women took up careers, and were exploited by being used in 'cheap' jobs such as clerking and school-teaching. The role of woman as wife and mother was vanishing with this change and with the rise of machines such as vacuum cleaners to relieve her of the burden of housework. Women were demanding the vote, and would get it; but something vital, Leacock argued, was being lost. 'No man ever said his prayers at the knees of a vacuum cleaner, or drew his first lessons in manliness and worth from the sweet old-fashioned stories that a vacuum-cleaner told.' (p. 58) Leacock firmly believed that a woman's place was in the home, and he had little respect for her ability at business or professional work; but his crotchety chauvinism is palliated by his concern for the decline of home and family life under the onslaught of the age of progress. The 'new' woman would not be free at all, but, like men, a slave to a harsh system of wage-contracts and poverty; and the home, which might have provided some stability and an alternative set of values, was being destroyed:

The home has passed, or at least is passing out of existence. In place of it is the 'apartment' — an incomplete thing, a mere part of something, where children are an intrusion, where hospitality is done through a caterer, and where Christmas is only the twenty-fifth of December. [p. 55]

In the ruthless system which defined people simply by their ability to produce and consume, not only must the lower class be forced to the poverty line and held there, but it must be stripped of those habits, rituals, and customs that were the anodynes of the bleak and bitter lives of working men; for these interfered with progress, work, and efficiency. Not only did a man lose his home and his family life, but even his mug of ale was to be snatched from his hand.

Prohibition, Leacock pointed out in 'The Tyranny of Prohibition,' was enacted in the name of morality by certain groups for the 'Benefit' of certain other groups; few who voted for it did so on the assumption that *they* might have to stop drinking! The South voted to keep liquor from the Blacks, farmers and shopkeepers voted each other dry, and employers supported it because they 'thought that drinkless men would work better.' (p. 68)

Thus all the ideas or institutions which might have put a brake on the human selfishness set loose by the rise of individualism, or might have modified or ameliorated its worst aspects, were in fact destroyed by progress. At the same time, Leacock was chronicling the corruption of politics and government, which were likewise succumbing to the blandishments of a material age. The ideas of materialism, individualism, and mastery of nature were supreme in North America. The result was a dynamic, but increasingly one-dimensional society, a society without critics, without opposition, in which man, pursuing his selfish individual ends in the name of an ideology which perpetuated injustice, headed for moral breakdown and social catastrophe. 'The new government of the money power,' he wrote in 1917,

was without a soul. It knew nothing of the ancient pride of place and race that dictated a certain duty towards those below. The creed that was embodied in the words *noblesse oblige* has vanished with the nobility. The plutocrat, unfettered by responsibility, seem[s] as rapacious and remorseless as the machinery that has made him.[37]

This depressing picture was given force and depth in Leacock's most ambitious works of fiction, *Arcadian Adventures with the Idle Rich* and *Sunshine Sketches of a Little Town*. In *Arcadian Adventures* the gloom of the essays is translated into a corrosive satire of an imaginary City in which the values of the age of progress have achieved untrammelled sway. The rich have amassed great wealth, and have arranged the City, and nature itself, according to their will. They live on the 'best' street at the top of the hill, where only 'the most expensive kind of birds'[38] sing in the trees. Their lives are spent at the Mausoleum Club, an artificial environment of rubber plants, electric lighting, white linen, and soft carpets. They are described as wholly predatory creatures, glaring at each other like greedy and suspicious animals. The slums are kept carefully hidden from them, though the rich are uncomfortably aware of their presence. In general the poor accept their lot, and share the values of the rich.

The plutocrats were not always the inhuman denizens of the Mausoleum Club. They lost their moral sense, taste, and capacity for love during their climb from the slums, or from Mariposa, where many of them originated. This process of transition is depicted in 'L'Envoi' of *Sunshine Sketches,* which connects the two books. We are told that when the plutocrat first came to the City from Mariposa to make his fortune, he dreamed of returning as a rich man to build a frame house on the main street. But when he made money, he built instead a sandstone house in the costlier part of the City, and forgot the small town. Many years later, he and the narrator are going home on the train to Mariposa. 'No,' the narrator tells him, 'don't bother to look at the reflection of your face in the window-pane shadowed by the night outside. Nobody could tell you now after all these years. Your face has changed in these long years of money-getting in the city.'[39] In other words, the rich master not only nature but themselves; they suppress all values non-essential to money-making, and identify themselves with what they make and do. In the process they cut themselves off from their own pasts, and from history in general. Life becomes an eternal 'now,' dynamic, fluid, in which everyone and everything is judged by present worth and utility, and discarded when these are gone.

The institutions which might have preserved a sense of the past are powerless in this society, and are captured and moulded by its values. The family is merely a group of people under the same roof, with the father making money, the mother pursuing pseudo-avocations, and sons and daughters seeking pleasure. The university, the churches, and the government are treated in more detail. In each case Leacock is careful not only to describe the institution, but to show how it got that way.

Plutoria University has grown from a quiet building under the elms to a modern knowledge factory with science buildings 'comparing favourably with the best departmental stores or factories in the City.'[40] President Boomer was once a fat little boy in a classical academy stuffing himself with Greek irregular verbs as he would have done with oysters. But he adapted himself to new ideas, made his peace with the businessmen, and now spends his days tearing down old buildings and throwing up new ones, firing professors, enlarging and changing the curriculum, and seeking new benefactions. He and his university survive, a significant accomplishment in a world which worships only survival and success, but the university is a mere parody of what it once was. The older ideal is represented by the pathetic figure of Dr McTeague, vainly trying to reconcile Hegel with St Paul, and being damned with the characteristic words of the age: 'He is not up to date.'[41]

Religion is likewise an empty shell. Both the churches on Plutoria Avenue climbed with their parishioners from the slums, losing their creeds along the way. The Episcopal rector is a nice young man whose sermons explain away hell, who performs 'society' weddings and funerals and never goes near the slums, who 'wears a little crucifix and dances the tango.'[42] The Presbyterian church retaliates by bringing in a hellfire-and-damnation minister who rails at the poor and puts on a good show until he is lured to another congregation by a better salary. The plutocrats solve this ruinous competition by a business-style merger of the churches; each member of the congregation is allowed to hold whatever doctrine he wishes, with disputed points to be settled by a majority vote of the shareholders.

Honesty in the politics of such a society is clearly impossible. A 'Clean Government' movement begins in response to the corruption of the City Council. With cynical clarity Leacock describes how the plutocrats capture the movement, use it to put their own men in power, and reward their civic virtue with coal and traction contracts, power and light franchises, and other good things.

Only once do nature and human goodness triumph over the mastery of Plutoria Avenue. Tomlinson, a poor back township farmer, becomes suddenly rich when gold is discovered on his land. He moves to the Grand Palaver Hotel where he and his family degenerate in unaccustomed and unwanted luxury. He decides to lose his fortune by investing in worthless stocks, but such is his reputation as a 'wizard of finance' that everything he touches jumps in value. Just as he is about to donate his money to the university, it is discovered that the gold claim was 'salted,' and the fortune is lost. Tomlinson and his family return to their farm and begin to remove the mining company's equipment. 'Nature reached out its hand and drew its coverlet of green over the grave of the vanished Eldorado.'[43]

Tomlinson had acquired his reputation as a 'wizard' by refusing to sell part of his land to the mining company because his father was buried there. The company, thinking that there must be more gold on that part of the land, increased their offer; the plutocrats thought this story of the father's grave merely a clever trick to get more money. Tomlinson and his farm survive the embrace of Plutoria Avenue, but only at the price of humiliation and poverty; this, Leacock implies, is a price most people will not and cannot pay.

The City of *Arcadian Adventures* is thus a kind of hell in which the rich, along with the poor and the professional classes, are compelled to exist in a state in which every decent emotion of man hides its opposite, in which, cut off from history, with everything judged by its money value and its utility, men go through the motions of being doctors, professors, ministers, lawyers, and businessmen, with little or no conception of what they are doing or why they are doing it, only that they must continue in order to survive. It is a jungle, but one without beauty or purpose. Leacock allows no affirmations in this book. Like Diogenes, he shines his lantern into every dark corner seeking honesty and finding only corruption and hypocrisy.

Is Mariposa any different? Of course, it is a happier and more innocent place, which has not yet become Plutoria Avenue. But fundamentally, both places believe in the same things: materialism, individualism, and mastery of nature. 'Ask any of its inhabitants if Mariposa isn't a busy, hustling, thriving town. ... ask any of them if they ever knew a more rushing go-ahead town than Mariposa,'[44] says the narrator. Mariposa is the boyhood home of the plutocrat; it is the historical antecedent of the City; and at present it is the satellite of the City, aping its values, styles, and ideas, and certainly no more high-minded in religion or in politics. 'It is not for nothing that Mr Leacock is a student of economics and sociology,' said the august *Review of Historical Publications Relating to Canada* (breaking this once its rule of never reviewing fiction):

he has been able to grasp many of the typical features of the Ontario town. ... Students of Canadian political conditions would do well to ponder Mr Leacock's account of the political career of Mr Josh Smith ... they will find it to contain more instructive matter than many a treatise of a more pretentious character.

Mariposans, Leacock seems to say, should enjoy the sunshine while they can.

What was Leacock's answer to this grim world he presented? Did he see it as inevitable that Mariposa should become Plutoria? Was *Arcadian Adventures* merely a warning, or was it Leacock's vision of a society that already existed? What did Professor Leacock want us to do?

In analyzing other people's panacaeas he again held up the lantern of Diogenes. Technocracy, or the rule of experts who would use the new machinery to ensure abundance and justice, was the solution reached by Veblen after a similar analysis of industrial society. Leacock rejected this solution because he felt that the technocrats, being themselves the products of a machine age, might be more efficient than the plutocrats, but would be no more humane. He had a deep fear of the dehumanizing effect of a dynamic technology; during the war and especially in the twenties he poured out a stream of sketches lampooning efficiency crazes, fads, and the worship of new inventions like the motor car, the movies, and the radio. Behind the fun lurked the fear that man was becoming the slave of his machines and his technique, and was losing his individuality and sense of purpose. Technocracy would simply aggravate the problem.

Likewise he rejected socialism, a creed whose full meaning Leacock never really understood. In his only scholarly discussion of it, a chapter in *Elements,* he treated it superficially, overstressing the utopians and giving Bellamy's *Looking Backward* far more attention than it deserved. Thereafter, in *The Unsolved Riddle* and elsewhere, he centred his discussions of socialism entirely on Bellamy's book. Even in the thirties he could never see socialism as anything but the misguided utopianism of middle-class idealists. He professed sympathy with socialism as he understood it, but feared that it would not 'work'; it would simply replace the rule of plutocrats with that of ignorant and selfish bosses, and like technocracy, it would place too much emphasis on technology and technique instead of on the human spirit. Often his criticisms of these two systems blended, for he felt that both would create a grey, lifeless world.

From all the analysis which has preceded, we can clearly see that Leacock was a conservative, indeed, a Tory. Surely, then, he looked

back to some long-dead golden age? The fact is, however, that Leacock strongly believed in certain kinds of progress, and declared that
no age in the past was better than his own. 'Only a false mediaevalism,' he said in *The Unsolved Riddle,* 'can paint the past in colours
superior to the present.' (p. 80) In 'Literature and Education in
America,' he concluded that North America's lack of culture may be
the price paid for the achievement of feeding, clothing, housing, and
educating its people; if this were the case, the price was not too high.
Elements is charged throughout with the assumption that history is a
story of scientific, economic, and social progress.

   This would seem a strange paradox. How can a man condemn the
results of the age of progress and believe in progress at the same
time? Some have suggested that this was an unresolved conflict in a
supremely eclectic mind, which set up an intellectual tension that
could only be resolved by humour.[46] There is truth in this, but the
paradox is not as large as it seems. Our clue is in the last section of
Elements, where Leacock examined and rejected 'Individualism' and
'Socialism' and came to the conclusion that 'The Modern State'
would be essentially individualistic, but would blend strong state
control to curb plutocratic excesses, regulate business in the public
interest (but not indulge in public ownership), and provide social
welfare services. It was implied that this was but one more step on a
road of progress which took men from the closed, hierarchical
poverty of the Middle Ages to the age of industrialism, and would
lead in the future to an age in which the power of machinery and the
mediaeval sense of social obligation would be combined.

   But while he believed in the possibility of this progress, Leacock
did not see it as automatic. Men had to make their own world. The
problem was that those agencies which might have transferred the
spirit of collectivism and provided the germ for the new society were
fatally weakened; therefore men had to be made aware of the shortcomings of individualism so that they could acquire the new spirit
which alone could make the new world function in the interests of
all and prevent social upheaval. '...[E]ven democracy,' he said in
1917, 'is valueless unless it can be inspired by the public virtue of
the citizen that raises him to the level of the privileges that he
enjoys. ... We must manage to create as the first requisite of our
commonwealth a different kind of spirit from that which has hitherto controlled us.'[47] The imperial movement would create such a

spirit of patriotism and duty to one's fellow man, but it could not do so alone. Here the artist came to the aid of the political economist. The only answer for a man who did not believe in Utopia, and could not take refuge in the past, was to hold up a mirror to men so that they could see themselves as they were and were becoming, and be convinced of the need for spiritual regeneration. This answer alone explains the extreme cynicism and bitterness of *Arcadian Adventures*. It was not about a real city, though like any artist Leacock had his models. It was a world of the not-too-distant future, a warning to men. That *Arcadian Adventures,* about a wholly fictional city, should have been set in the United States, and that *Sunshine Sketches,* about a demonstrably real town, should have been set in Canada, shows that on the eve of the Great War Leacock believed that there was still hope, if he could only reach his audience in time.

The wartime experience of Canada and the United States made Leacock more optimistic, for it seemed to bring into being the sort of political change and spiritual revival he desired. Canadians united in the spirit of patriotism. Imperial unity began to take on reality, as men and supplies poured across the sea to a beleaguered motherland in larger flotillas than the world had yet seen. Thousands laid down their lives in an unprecedented display of self-sacrifice. Old economic theories were discarded as governments took an active role in controlling production and distribution, regulating business and mediating labour disputes, conserving resources, and supervising railways. The state became a war machine, directing the citizen in his consumption and use of goods. The old free-wheeling individualism was gone, Leacock hoped forever. Particularly Leacock supported conscription as the embodiment of this new national solidarity; but he carried the idea further and called for conscription of wealth as well as of men. Only a nation in which every citizen was giving of his goods until none were left, he argued, could order a soldier to die for it. If people would not voluntarily contribute, a government 'of iron power' should make them. Canada, he said, now knew her destiny. 'That is the supreme meaning of the war to us. ... It is the glad cry of a people that have found themselves.' [48]

Leacock fervently hoped that the United States would come into the war, joining the British Empire in the great struggle and experiencing the same purifying influences Canada was receiving. He bitterly attacked Wilson's neutrality and did all he could to dispose

the Americans favourably to the British cause. When the United
States did enter the war, Leacock's delight knew no bounds. Never
again in his writings was he hostile to that country. His feelings are
clearly expressed in a 1917 sketch, 'Father Knickerbocker, a
Fantasy.' The symbol of New York escorts the narrator through the
city's night clubs, orders a big meal with drinks, eyes the girls lascivi-
ously, and wallows in luxury. As the narrator is about to conclude
that Knickerbocker is hopelessly lost in self-indulgence, the booming
of far-off guns is heard and the whole picture changes.

> 'War!' cried Father Knickerbocker, rising to his full height, stern and
> majestic and shouting in a stentorian tone that echoed through the
> great room. 'War! War! To your places, every one of you! Be done
> with your idle luxury! Out with the glare of your lights! Begone you
> painted women and worthless men!'...
>   And I knew that a great nation had cast aside the bonds of sloth
> and luxury, and was girding itself to join in the fight for the free
> democracy of all mankind.[49]

If the land of *Arcadian Adventures* could rise to its duty, could
catch the spirit of patriotism and valour and sacrifice, then surely all
things were possible.

The Unsolved Riddle, then, was written with mixed feelings.
There was on the one hand the fear that the idealism and sacrifice of
the war, perverted into 'National Hysteria,' could lead to chaos; but
on the other hand there was the profounder hope that this spirit,
now finally roused to its duty, could be channelled into the building
of a new world 'in which there may be achieved some part of all that
has been dreamed in the age-long passion for social justice.' (p. 75)
The book was in a sense a final acceptance by Leacock both of
industrial society and of the ability of men of good will to resolve
their own problems. He had preached at them, complained to them,
satirized them; now he reasoned with them. The message is basically
the same. There is no Utopia. Leacock makes proposals to improve
the situation. '[T]he government of every country,' he concludes,
'ought to supply work and pay for the unemployed, maintenance for
the infirm and aged, and education and opportunity for the children'
(p. 140), though '[t]he vast mass of human industrial effort must
still lie outside of the immediate control of the government.'

(p. 141) But even this modest programme of social benefit, he cautions, 'must depend at every stage on the force of public spirit and public morality that inspires it.' (p. 136)

But Diogenes must have the last word on a point this hopeful. In an unpublished essay in which Leacock outlined similar programmes to those advocated in *The Unsolved Riddle,* he confessed to misgivings:

I don't ... say that such a picture of the new regime is altogether an attractive one. To those of us who grew up under the older dispensation and, with all its faults, flourished under it, the outlook is perhaps distressing. This new world, with its fussy interfering government in which everybody's business is everybody else's business, in which everybody works and nobody drinks, where a tiresome and orderly efficiency takes the place of a largehearted and genial wastefulness — such a world, I say, may prove to many of us but a sorry place to live in. But a generation is a passing thing. Our little taper flickers and dies out, and new lights appear. ... Perhaps in a broader illumination the latter-comers will look back with something like horror to what seems the dark appalling confusion + injustice in which we dwelt.[50]

And so the humorist served notice that though he accepted the new world, he reserved the right to laugh at it, too.

Stephen Leacock was part of that curious and perhaps indigenously Canadian species which has been given the name of 'Red Tory.'[51] Troubled by the intellectual and physical results of the age of progress, he refused to live in the past, yet feared the social upheaval rapid change might cause. While we may feel that at times Leacock doubted too much and hoped too little, we cannot question his sincerity in ardently promoting those measures of reform which he felt were within the limits of the possible. His imperialism, his essays, and his best humour all show various aspects of this social concern, and each serves to deepen our understanding of the others. Leacock the humorist no less than Leacock the man is not fully comprehensible unless his intellectual preoccupations and his relationship to the age in which he lived are clearly understood.

Literary critics for a generation have vexed themselves with the question: Why didn't Leacock write the Great Canadian Novel?[52] From a historical viewpoint, several other questions are equally relevant. Why didn't he go into politics? ('I think that if he had chosen to go into politics, he could easily have become prime minister,' said his student and colleague Eugene Forsey;[53] Leacock on several occasions was offered safe seats but declined, though he did jokingly say that he would accept a seat in the Canadian Senate at a moment's notice.) Why didn't he continue as an essayist writing witty and biting pieces on all phases of Canadian life, like the ones in this book? Why didn't he fulfil the promise of *Elements* and become a great political scientist if not a great economist? The answers to all these questions have been suggested in this introduction; the point is that Leacock never achieved that supreme excellence which was potentially his in almost everything he did. By focussing attention exclusively on the question of novel-writing, these critics are adopting a highly arbitrary standard for judging human greatness, even literary greatness, and they are forcing upon the events of Leacock's life an order of importance which was not his.

Leacock the man cannot be brushed aside in favour of Leacock the humorist. Leacock the man was concerned with social and political problems, deeply involved in the affairs of his age. He used all his many and varied talents to define these problems to himself and his contemporaries, and to advocate solutions to them as persuasively as he knew how. Only after 1922 did he see himself primarily as a humorist; before this time, in large measure, his humour was but one of the weapons he brought to bear on social problems. He could not see his humour, or any of his other talents, in a vacuum, existing apart from the audiences he wanted to reach or the problems he wanted to solve. Whatever may be the relative literary merits of these writings, however much critics with their hindsight may lament that his genius moved in what seems to them a false direction, we must understand that, given the man Leacock was and the times in which he lived, the path which led from *Elements* through 'Greater Canada,' the essays, *Sunshine Sketches* and *Arcadian Adventures,* and the wartime humour and propaganda, to *The Unsolved Riddle,* was the only one he could have followed.

Even had novel-writing been high on Leacock's list of priorities, his genius probably did not lie in that direction. H.A. Innis, Canada's greatest economist, rightly remarks that the social sciences gave Leacock 'an interest in institutions rather than persons.'[54] The truth of this can best be illustrated by examining the two books which are alleged to be the sign that Leacock was moving toward the writing of novels: *Sunshine Sketches* and *Arcadian Adventures.* In both books the human characters, however subtly and sympathetically drawn, serve primarily to illustrate the workings of social institutions. The real main characters which emerge are not any of the people, but Mariposa and the City themselves. And this was exactly what Leacock intended. What indication is there that he wanted to say more, or had more to say, about people or about humanity? Novel writing with its demands for psychological insight and rounded characterization would have been foreign both to Leacock's genius and to his major concerns.[55] If we really want to understand him we must cease to fantasize about the novelist who might have been and concentrate our attention on the social scientist who was; for it was a social scientist, not an embryo novelist, who wrote Leacock's best humour.

If we are thus forced to accept Leacock as a relatively stunted plant instead of the mighty oak which might (or might not) have been, there are compensations. To the historian, studying Leacock's many-faceted life against the backdrop of a dramatic and formative period in our history, Leacock's failure to write the Great Canadian Novel or to do any of the other things he might have done is no tragedy; it could be so only to those preoccupied with works and not with lives. If he had specialized more in any field Leacock might have left a more lasting monument, but he would have been a lesser man.

As a social scientist, with forays into politics, imperialism, and humour, Leacock stands out in the intellectual history of Canada. He anticipated several trends in later Canadian thought: not only the 'Red Toryism' of Grant, but the preoccupation with technology and its relation to the Canadian identity which marked the later career of Innis and has produced Marshall McLuhan. Leacock was one of the first Canadian academics to fuse the insights of the American progressives with the British and Canadian conservative tradition in order to develop an analysis of the United States and North American society which was uniquely Canadian. He needs no apology for either his humour or his social science. 'There are simple minds,' said

Harold Innis, 'which adopt Leacock's own statement that political economists regarded him as a humorist and that humorists regarded him as a political economist. According to the lights of this economist [Innis] he did much to save the soul of both in a period in which they were in grave danger.'[56] Leacock the social scientist richly deserves Robertson Davies' description of Leacock the humorist: 'A great countryman of ours: a man to thank God for.'[57]

NOTES

1 Robert M. Bingay, 'The Angels Laughing,' reprinted from the Detroit *Free Press* in the Orillia *Packet and Times,* 6 Apr. 1944
2 McGill University Archives, Peterson Papers, file 70, Parkin to Peterson, 19 Jan. 1900
3 *Ibid.*
4 Peterson Papers, file 70, Leacock to Peterson, 18 Jan. 1900; 5 May 1900
5 An interesting discussion of Veblen (which shows the debt of *The Unsolved Riddle*'s opening chapters to him), and of Soddy and The Technocrats, is found in *My Discovery of the West,* 171-6.
6 McGill University Archives, Peterson Letterbooks, I, 408, Peterson to James Mavor, 26 Apr. 1900
7 University of Toronto Archives, James Loudon Papers, James Mavor, notes on applicants for Associate Professor of Political Science [1905]
8 J.A. Hobson, *Canada Today* (London 1906), 4
9 Peterson Papers, file 65, Grey to Peterson, 4 Nov. 1905
10 As an example of the reaction to Leacock's lectures and the debate stirred by them, at one of his lectures Sir Frederick Borden, Minister of Militia, stood up and disagreed with his contention that the Monroe Doctrine was not a protection for Canada and questioned Leacock's statement of the need for a navy. Leacock replied on the spot, and the resulting debate was the subject of much newspaper controversy and an exchange in the House of Commons. See, for example, the Orillia *Packet,* 22 Mar. 1906.
11 See the Orillia *Packet,* 7 Mar. 1907.

12 This description of Leacock's speaking style is gleaned from newspaper reports too numerous to mention. Two articles give the best
picture of Leacock as orator in the years before the war: C. Lentern
Sibley, 'Stephen Leacock,' *Globe*, 28 Dec. 1912, and Trevor Lautens
Lautens, reprinted from the Hamilton *Spectator* in the Orillia *Packet
and Times*, Article #3, 27 Aug. 1956.
13 Peterson Papers, file 65, Grey to Peterson, 30 Jan. 1906 (first
quote) and re imperial missionary) *ibid.*, file 46, Grey to Peterson,
25 Mar. 1907
14 Richard Jebb was a leading English imperialist propagandist who had
travelled all over the empire and the world (1897-1901), and had
achieved wide fame with his book, *Studies in Colonial Nationalism*
(1905). In 1906 he visited Canada, Australia, and South Africa.
Other books by Jebb include *The Britannic Question* (1913) and
The Imperial Conference (1911).
15 Peterson Papers, file 46, Leacock to Peterson, 24 May 1907
16 Peterson Papers, file 65, Grey to Peterson, 30 Jan. 1906
17 'John Bull, Farmer,' Orillia *Packet,* 30 May 1907
18 John S. Ewart, 'A Perplexed Imperialist,' 90. *The Canadian Annual
Review* for 1907 (p. 374) attributes the statement to L.V. Harcourt.
19 Peterson Letterbooks, XI, 226, 18 July 1907, Peterson to Leacock;
XII, 12, 16 Nov. 1907, Peterson to Leacock. Interestingly, Rudyard
Kipling and Richard Jebb liked Leacock's article and thought it was
just what was needed.
20 Quoted in J. Eayrs, 'The Round Table Movement in Canada, 1909-
1920,' in C. Berger, ed., *Imperial Relations in the Age of Laurier*
(Toronto 1969), 67
21 Canadian Home Manufacturers Association Minute Book, in the
possession of Professor R. Craig Brown, University of Toronto
22 'The Great Victory in Canada,' 392, See also the Orillia *Packet*
during the election period.
23 McGill University Library, Rare Books Department, Stephen
Leacock Collection, Mss, Box 7, 'War Time in Canada'
24 *Ibid.*, in box with Mss 'Arcadian Adventures,' 'The Fallacies and
Failures of the Income Tax,' and Box 14, 'The Present Crisis.' The
attack on public ownership of railways is well known: see for the
fullest statement of his position, *My Discovery of the West*, ch. 13,
265-77. Leacock never relented in his attack on the CNR, and was a

close personal friend of Sir Edward Beatty, Chancellor of McGill and President of the CPR.

25 See *Canadian Annual Review*, 1921, 554-5, and Sir John Willison, 'From Month to Month,' *Canadian Magazine*, LVII, 1964-5.

26 'Sir Wilfrid Laurier's Victory,' 828

27 'The Asiatic Problem in the British Empire,' 6

28 'The Union of South Africa,' 503

29 'Laurier's Victory,' 833

30 *Ibid.*, 832

31 'Canada and the Immigration Problem,' 323, 327

32 'Laurier's Victory,' 831

33 'Perplexed Imperialist,' 90

34 'Democracy and Social Progress,' 17

35 'Andrew Macphail,' in *The Boy I Left Behind Me*, 138

36 *Lament for a Nation* (Toronto 1965). See p. 56; 'To modern political theory...' to end of paragraph. See also pp. 64, 66. The similarities between Leacock and Grant in their views of liberalism and progress are striking.

37 'Democracy and Social Progress,' 15-16

38 *Arcadian Adventures* (New Canadian Library), 1

39 *Sunshine Sketches* (New Canadian Library), 152

40 *Arcadian Adventures*, 39

41 *Ibid.*, 104

42 *Ibid.*, 102

43 *Ibid.*, 55-6

44 *Sunshine Sketches*, 2-3

45 G.M. Wrong and H.H. Langton, eds., *Review of Historical Publications Relating to Canada*, XVII, 111, 112

46 The point is most explicitly made in Donald Cameron, *Faces of Leacock* (Toronto 1967), 3-5; 16-7. F.W. Watt, 'Critic or Entertainer: Leacock and the Growth of Materialism,' hints at this point too. He analyzes Leacock's refusal to glorify the past and his criticism of the present, and suggests that humour was Leacock's way of making life acceptable to his audiences and himself. Leacock is thus both critic and entertainer. I think that H.A. Innis is closer to the truth in his analysis of the origins of Leacock's humorous urge when he writes: 'The social scientist and especially the student of political economy is compelled to make his peace with satire or humour. The callous

vulgarity which characterizes the medical profession is paralleled by cynicism in the social sciences.' Innis, 'Stephen Butler Leacock,' 221

47 'Democracy and Social Progress,' 31-2

48 McGill Library, Leacock Mss, Box 7, 'War Time in Canada.' See also, for Leacock's analysis of the economic implications of the war and their effect on the postwar world, 'Old Theories and New Facts — The Economic World After the War,' unpublished ms, Box 14, and 'The Economic Aspect of War,' *Journal of the Canadian Bankers' Association*, XXIV, 302-15.

49 *Frenzied Fiction* (New Canadian Library), 33-4

50 'Old Theories and New Facts — The Economic World After the War'

51 *Vide* G. Horowitz, *Canadian Labour in Politics* (Toronto 1968), 3-57

52 The best summary of the various positions in this debate, as well as the most persuasive (but in my mind unconvincing) argument that Leacock could have been a novelist, is found in D. Cameron, *Faces of Leacock,* 138-54.

53 *CBC Times,* 8-14 June 1958, 3

54 Innis, 'Stephen Butler Leacock,' 223

55 Leacock himself recognized that he was not primarily interested in writing about people except as they represented types or the working of human institutions. 'I can invent characters quite easily,' he once wrote, 'but I have no notion as to how to make things happen to them. Indeed I see no reason why anything should. I could write awfully good short stories if it were only permissible, merely to introduce some extremely original character and at the end of two pages announce that at this point a brick fell on his head and killed him. If there was room for a school of literature of this kind I should offer to head it.' Quoted in Innis, 'Stephen Butler Leacock,' 224

56 *Ibid.,* 226

57 Robertson Davies, 'Stephen Leacock,' in C.T. Bissell, ed., *Our Living Tradition,* First Series (Toronto 1957), 149

Selected Bibliography

I SELECTED ARTICLES BY LEACOCK WRITTEN BEFORE 1921 WHICH
   ARE NOT REPRINTED IN BOOK FORM

1906
'The Imperial Crisis,' in *Addresses Delivered Before the Canadian
Club of Toronto,* season 1905-6 (Toronto [1906]), 114-18

1907
'Greater Canada: An Appeal,' *University Magazine,* VI, 132-41
'John Bull, Farmer,' Orillia *Packet,* 30 May 1907
'Responsible Government in the British Colonial System,' *American
Political Science Review,* I, 355-92
'Education and Empire Unity,' *Empire Club Speeches, Being Ad-
dresses Delivered Before the Empire Club of Canada During its
Session of 1906-07* (Toronto 1907), 276-305

1908
'The Limitations of Federal Government,' American Political
Science Association *Proceedings,* V, 37-52
'The Asiatic Problem in the British Empire,' Orillia *Packet,* 21 May
1908

1909
'Canada and the Monroe Doctrine,' *University Magazine,* VIII,
351-74
'Sir Wilfrid Laurier's Victory,' *National Review* (London), LII,
826-33
'The Political Achievement of Robert Baldwin,' *Addresses Delivered
Before the Canadian Club of Ottawa, 1903-1909* (Ottawa 1910),
161-4
'The International Tax Conference and Canadian Public Finance,'
University of Toronto Monthly, IX, 8-12

1910
'The Union of South Africa,' *American Political Science Review,* IV,
498-507

1911

'What Shall We Do About the Navy?' *University Magazine*, X, 535-53

'Canada and the Immigration Problem,' *National Review*, LVII, 316-27

'The Great Victory in Canada,' *National Review*, LVII, 381-92

1913

'The University and Business,' *University Magazine*, XII, 540-9

'The Canadian Senate and the Naval Bill,' *National Review*, LXI, 986-98

'The High Cost of Living,' *Addresses Delivered Before the Canadian Club of Montreal*, season 1913-14. ([n.p.] [n.d.]), 44-52

1914

'The American Attitude,' *University Magazine*, XIII, 595-7

'The Canadian Balance of Trade,' *Journal of the Canadian Bankers' Association*, XXII, 165-77

1916

'Is Permanent Peace Possible?,' *Maclean's*, XXIX (August), 7-8, 77-99; (October), 12-13, 92-3

'The Economic Aspect of War,' *Journal of the Canadian Bankers' Association*, XXIV, 302-15

1917

'Our National Organization for the War,' in J.O. Miller, ed., *The New Era in Canada...* (London 1917), 409-21

'Democracy and Social Progress,' *ibid.*, 13-33

'Ten Million Dollars For the Asking,' *Maclean's*, XXX (March), 9-12

1918

'Inside the Tank,' *Maclean's*, XXXI (January), 38-40

1919

'The Tyranny of Prohibition,' *Living Age*, CCCII, 301-6

II BOOKS

A Pre-1921

Elements of Political Science (Boston 1906; rev. 1921)

Baldwin, Lafontaine, Hincks: Responsible Government (Toronto 1907)

Adventures of the Far North, A Chronicle of the Frozen Seas (Toronto 1914)

The Dawn of Canadian History: A Chronicle of Aboriginal Canada and the Coming of the White Man (Toronto 1914)

The Mariner of St Malo; A Chronicle of the Voyages of Jacques Cartier (Toronto 1914)

Essays and Literary Studies (Toronto 1916). The first four essays in this book were published in the *University Magazine* in 1910, 1910, 1909, and 1907 respectively. 'The Woman Question' was first published in *Maclean's* in 1915.

The Hohenzollerns in America: With the Bolsheviks in Berlin and Other Impossibilities (London & New York 1919)

The Unsolved Riddle of Social Justice (Toronto 1920)

B *The following books are easily available in the McClelland & Stewart New Canadian Library Series, so that full bibliographical information is not necessary:*

Literary Lapses (1910)

Nonsense Novels (1911)

Sunshine Sketches of a Little Town (1912)

Behind the Beyond (1913)

Arcadian Adventures With the Idle Rich (1914)

Moonbeams From the Larger Lunacy (1915)

Further Foolishness (1917)

Frenzied Fiction (1919)

My Discovery of England (1922)

Winnowed Wisdom (1926)

Short Circuits (1928)

My Remarkable Uncle and Other Sketches (1941)

Last Leaves (1945)

C *The student with a special interest in Leacock's ideas of politics, economics, education, and history, should consult the following books published after 1922:*

Afternoons in Utopia: Tales of the New Time (Toronto [1932])
Canada and the Sea (Montreal 1944)
Canada: The Foundations of its Future (Montreal 1941)
Economic Prosperity in the British Empire (Toronto 1930)
Here Are My Lectures and Stories (New York 1937)
My Discovery of the West: A Discussion of East and West in Canada
(Toronto 1937)
*Too Much College: or Education Eating Up Life, With Kindred
Essays in Education and Humour* (New York 1939)
*The Pursuit of Knowledge: A Discussion of Freedom and Compul-
sion in Education* (New York [c. 1934])
*Our Heritage of Liberty; Its Origin, Its Achievement, Its Crisis: A
Book for War Time* (London [1942])

III   WORKS ABOUT LEACOCK

A *Books*
Cameron, D. *Faces of Leacock: An Appreciation* (Toronto 1967)
Curry, R. *Stephen Leacock, Humorist and Humanist* (Garden City,
NY 1959)
Davies, R. *Stephen Leacock* (Toronto [1970])
Kimball, E. *The Man in the Panama Hat* (Toronto [1970])
Legate, D. *Stephen Leacock: A Biography* (Toronto 1970)
MacArthur, P. *Stephen Leacock* (Toronto [1925])

See also:
Berger, C. *The Sense of Power: Studies in the Ideas of Canadian
Imperialism* (Toronto 1970)

B *Articles*
Ewart, J.S. 'A Perplexed Imperialist,' *Queen's Quarterly*, XV, 90-100
Caldwell, W. 'Impressions of Ontario V: A Visit to a Canadian
Author,' *Canadian Magazine*, LIX, 55-60
Innis, H. 'Stephen Butler Leacock,' *Canadian Journal of Economics
and Political Science*, X, 216-30
Bissell, C. 'Haliburton, Leacock and the American Humourous (sic)
Tradition,' *Canadian Literature* 39 (winter 1969), 5-19
Watt, F.W. 'Critic or Entertainer? Stephen Leacock and the Growth
of Materialism,' *Canadian Literature* 5 (summer 1960), 33-42

Cook, G.R. 'Stephen Leacock and the Age of Plutocracy,' in John S. Moir, ed., *Character and Circumstance: Essays in Honour of Donald Grant Creighton* (Toronto 1970), 163-81

c *Bibliography*
Lomer, G.H. *Stephen Leacock: A Check-List and Index of His Writings* (Ottawa 1954)

The social criticism of Stephen Leacock

Greater Canada: an appeal

NOW, IN THIS month of April, when the ice is leaving our rivers, the ministers of Canada take ship for this the fourth Colonial Conference at London. What do they go to do? Nay, rather what shall we bid them do? We – the six million people of Canada, unvoiced, untaxed, in the Empire, unheeded in the councils of the world – we, the six million colonials sprawling our over-suckled infancy across a continent – what shall be our message to the motherland? Shall we still whine of our poverty, still draw imaginary pictures of our thin herds shivering in the cold blasts of the North, their shepherds huddled for shelter in the log cabins of Montreal and Toronto? Shall we still beg the good people of England to bear yet a little longer, for the poor peasants of their colony, the burden and heat of the day? Shall our ministers rehearse this worn-out fiction of our 'acres of snow,' and so sail home again, still untaxed, to the smug approval of the oblique politicians of Ottawa? Or, shall we say to the people of England, 'The time has come; we know and realize our country. We will be your colony no longer. Make us one with you in an Empire, Permanent and Indivisible.'

This last alternative means what is commonly called Imperialism. It means a united system of defence, an imperial navy for whose support somehow or other the whole Empire shall properly contribute, and with it an imperial authority in whose power we all may share. To many people in Canada this imperialism is a tainted word. It is too much associated with a truckling subservience to English people and English ideas and the silly swagger of the hop-o'-my-thumb junior officer. But there is and must be for the true future of our country, a higher and more real imperialism than this – the imperialism of the plain man at the plough and the clerk in the counting house, the imperialism of any decent citizen that demands for this country its proper place in the councils of the Empire and in the destiny of the world. In this sense, imperialism means but the realization of a Greater Canada, the recognition of a wider citizenship.

I, that write these lines, am an Imperialist because I will not be a Colonial. This Colonial status is a worn-out, by-gone thing. The sense and feeling of it has become harmful to us. It limits the ideas, and circumscribes the patriotism of our people. It impairs the mental vigor and narrows the outlook of those that are reared and educated in our midst. The English boy reads of England's history and its glories as his own; it is *his* navy that fought at Camperdown and Trafalgar, *his* people that have held fast their twenty miles of sea eight hundred years against a continent. He learns at his fire-side and at his school, among his elders and his contemporaries, to regard all this as part of himself; something that he, as a fighting man, may one day uphold, something for which as a plain citizen he shall every day gladly pay, something for which in any capacity it may one day be his high privilege to die. How little of this in Canada! Our paltry policy teaches the Canadian boy to detach himself from the England of the past, to forget that Camperdown and Copenhagen and the Nile are ours as much as theirs, that this navy of the Empire is ours too, ours in its history of the past, ours in its safe-guard of the present.

If this be our policy and plan, let us complete our teaching to our children. Let us inscribe it upon the walls of our schools, let us write it in brass upon our temples that for the Navy which made us and which defends us, we pay not a single penny, we spare not a solitary man. Let us add to it, also, that the lesson may bear fruit, this 'shelter theory' of Canada now rampant in our day; that Canada, by some reason of its remoteness from European sin and its proximity to American republicanism, is sheltered from that flail of war with which God tribulates the other peoples of the world, sheltered by the Monroe Doctrine, by President Roosevelt and his battleships, sheltered, I know not how, but sheltered somehow so that we may forget the lean, eager patriotism and sacrifice of a people bred for war, and ply in peace the little craft of gain and greed. So grows and has grown the Canadian boy in his colonial status, dissociated from the history of the world, cut off from the larger patriotism, colourless in his ideas. So grows he till in some sly way his mind opens to the fence-rail politics of his country side, with its bribed elections and its crooked votes – not patriotism but 'politics,' maple-leaf politics, by which money may be made and places and profit fall in a golden shower.

Some time ago Theodore Roosevelt, writing with the pardonable irresponsibility of a Police Commissioner of New York and not as President of the United States, said of us here in Canada, that the American feels towards the Canadian the good-natured condescension that is felt by the free-born man for the man that is not free. Only recently one of the most widely circulated of American

magazines, talking in the same vein, spoke of us Canadians as a
'subject people.' These are, of course, the statements of extravagance
and ignorance; but it is true, none the less, that the time has come to
be done with this *colonial* business, done with it once and forever.
We cannot in Canada continue as we are. We must become something greater or something infinitely less. We can no longer be an
appanage and outlying portion of something else. Canada, as a
colony, was right enough in the days of good old Governor Simcoe,
when your emigrant officer sat among the pine stumps of his Canadian clearing and reared his children in the fear of God and in the
love of England — right enough then, wrong enough and destructive
enough now. We cannot continue as we are. In the history of every
nation as of every man there is no such thing as standing still. There
is no pause upon the path of progress. There is no stagnation but the
hush of death.

And for this progress, this forward movement, what is there first
to do? How first unravel this vexed skein of our colonial and imperial relations? This, first of all. We must realize, and the people of
England must realize, the inevitable greatness of Canada. This is not
a vain-glorious boast. This is no rhodomontade. It is simple fact.
Here stand we, six million people, heirs to the greatest legacy in the
history of mankind, owners of half a continent, trustees, under God
Almighty, for the fertile solitudes of the west. A little people, few in
numbers, say you? Ah, truly such a little people! Few as the people
of the Greeks that blocked the mountain gates of Europe to the
march of Asia, few as the men of Rome that built a power to
dominate the world, nay, scarce more numerous than they in England
whose beacons flamed along the cliffs a warning to the heavy gal-
leons of Spain. Aye, such a little people, but growing, growing,
growing, with a march that shall make us ten millions to-morrow,
twenty millions in our children's time and a hundred millions ere yet
the century runs out. What say you to Fort Garry, a stockaded fort
in your father's day, with its hundred thousand of to-day and its half
a million souls of the to-morrow? What think you, little river
Thames, of our great Ottawa that flings its foam eight hundred
miles? What does it mean when science has moved us a little further
yet, and the wheels of the world's work turn with electric force?
What sort of asset do you think then our melting snow and the
roaring river-flood of our Canadian spring shall be to us? What say

you, little puffing steam-fed industry of England, to the industry of Coming Canada. Think you, you can heave your coal hard enough, sweating and grunting with your shovel to keep pace with the snow-fed cataracts of the north? Or look, were it but for double conviction, at the sheer extent and size of us. Throw aside, if you will, the vast districts of the frozen north, confiscate, if you like, Ungava still snow-covered and unknown, and let us talk of the Canada that we know, south of the sixtieth parallel, south of your Shetland Islands, south of the Russian Petersburg and reaching southward thence to where the peach groves of Niagara bloom in the latitude of northern Spain. And of all this take only our two new provinces, twin giants of the future, Alberta and Saskatchewan. Three decades ago this was the 'great lone land,' the frozen west, with its herds of bison and its Indian tepees, known to you only in the pictured desolation of its unending snow; now crossed and inter-crossed with railways, settled 400 miles from the American frontier, and sending north and south the packets of its daily papers from its two provincial capitals. And of this country, fertile as the corn plains of Hungary, and the crowded flats of Belgium, do you know the size? It is this. Put together the whole German Empire, the republic of France and your England and Scotland, and you shall find place for them in our two new provinces. Or take together across the boundary from us, the States of Maine, New Hampshire, Vermont, Massachusetts, Rhode Island, and Connecticut — all the New England States and with them all the Middle States of the North — New York, New Jersey, Pennsylvania, Delaware, Ohio, Indiana, Michigan, Illinois, and Wisconsin, till you have marked a space upon the map from the Atlantic to the Mississippi and from the Ohio to the lakes — all these you shall put into our two new provinces and still find place for England and for Scotland in their boundaries.

This then for the size and richness of our country. Would that the soul and spirit of its people were commensurate with its greatness. For here as yet we fail. Our politics, our public life and thought, rise not to the level of our opportunity. The mud-bespattered politicians of the trade, the party men and party managers, give us in place of patriotic statescraft the sordid traffic of a tolerated jobbery. For bread, a stone. Harsh is the cackle of the little turkey-cocks of Ottawa, fighting the while as they feather their mean nests of sticks and mud, high on their river bluff. Loud sings the little Man of the Province, crying his petty Gospel of Provincial Rights, grudging the

gift of power, till the cry spreads and town hates town and every
hamlet of the country side shouts for its share of plunder and of
pelf. This is the tenor of our politics, carrying as its undertone the
voice of the black-robed sectary, with narrow face and shifting eyes,
snarling still with the bigotry of a by-gone day. This is the spirit that
we must purge. This is the demon we must exorcise; this the disease,
the canker-worm of corruption, bred in the indolent securities of
peace, that must be burned from us in the pure fire of an Imperial
patriotism, that is no theory but a passion. This is our need, our
supreme need of the Empire – not for its ships and guns, but for the
greatness of it, the soul of it, aye for the very danger of it.

Of our spirit, then, it is not well. Nor is it well with the spirit of
those in England in their thoughts of us. Jangling are they these
twenty years over little Ireland that makes and unmakes ministries,
and never a thought of Canada; jangling now over their Pantaloon
Suffragettes and their Swaddled Bishops, wondering whether they
shall still represent their self-willed Lords nose for nose in the councils of the Empire or whether they may venture now to scale them
down, putting one nose for ten. One or ten, what does it matter, so
there is never a voice to speak for Canada? Can they not see, these
people of England, that the supreme English Question now is the
question of Canada: that this Conference of the year of grace 1907
might, if it would, make for us the future of the Empire? Or will
they still regard us, poor outlying sheltered people of Canada, as
something alien and apart, sending us ever of their youngest and
silliest to prate in easy arrogance of 'home,' earning the livelihood
their island cannot give, still snapping at the hand that feeds them?

And what then can this Colonial Conference effect after all, it is
asked? Granting, for argument's sake, the spirit of the people that
might prove it, our willingness to pay, their willingness to give us
place and power, what can be done? Hard indeed is the question.
Hard even to the Ready Man in the Street with his glib solution of
difficulties; harder still to the thoughtful; hardest of all to those who
will not think. For if we pay for this our Navy that even now
defends us, and yet speak not in the councils at Westminster, then is
that Taxation without Representation; straightway the soul of the
Anglo-Saxon stands aghast; the grim deaths-head of King John grins
in the grave, while the stout ghost of old Ben Franklin hovers again
upon our frontier holding in its hand the proffer of independence.

But if you admit us to your councils, what then? Ah, then indeed an awful thing befalls! Nothing less than the remaking of your constitution, with a patching and a re-building of it, till the nature-growth of precedent and custom is shaped in the clumsy artifice of clause and schedule, powers and prohibitions, measured and marked off with the yard-stick of the *ultra-vires* attorney. This surely is worse than ever. This perhaps you might have done, save for the bare turn of a majority, for Irksome Ireland. But for Uncomplaining Canada, not so.

So there we stand, we and you, pitched fast upon the horns of a dilemma. You cannot tax us, since you will not represent us. We cannot be represented because we will not be taxed. So we stand stock still, like the donkey in the philosophic fable, balanced between two bales of hay, nibbling neither right nor left. So are we like to stand, till some one of us, some of you and us, shall smite the poor donkey of our joint stupidity there where it most profits that a donkey shall be smitten, and bid it move!

Yet is the difficulty perhaps not impossible of solution. The thing to be achieved is there. The task is yours to solve, men of the council table. Find us a way whereby the burden and the power shall fall on all alike; a way whereby, taxed, we shall still be free men, free of the Imperial citizenship, and your historic constitution unshattered in the progress. Is it then so difficult? We come of a race that has solved much, has so often achieved the impossible. Look back a little in the ages to where ragged Democracy howls around the throne of defiant Kingship. This is a problem that we have solved, joining the dignity of Kingship with the power of democracy; this, too, by the simplest of political necromancy, the trick of which we now expound in our schools, as the very alphabet of political wisdom. Or look back to where the scaffolds of a bigot nation run with blood for the sake of rival creeds that know not yet the simple code of toleration, to be framed now in an easy statute with an artful stroke of a pen. Have we done all this and shall we balk at this poor colonial question? At it then, like men, shrewd representatives of Ottawa and Westminster, trained in the wisdom of the ages. Listen not to those who would block the way with a *non possumus* on this side, a *non volumus* on that. Find us a way, shew us a plan, a mere beginning if you will, a widow's mite of contribution, a mere whispering of representation, but something that shall trace for us the future path of Empire.

Nor is guidance altogether lacking in the task. For at least the signs of the times are written large as to what the destiny of Canada shall *not* be. Not as it is – not on this *colonial* footing, can it indefinitely last. There are those who tell us that it is best to leave well alone, to wait for the slow growth, the evolution of things. For herein lies the darling thought of the wisdom of the nineteenth century, in ·this same Evolution, this ready-made explanation of all things; hauled over from the researches of the botanist to meet the lack of thought of the philosopher. Whatever is, is: whatever will be, will be – so runs its silly creed. Therefore let everything be, that is: and all that shall be, shall be! This is but the wisdom of the fool, wise after the fact. For the solution of our vexed colonial problem this profits nothing. We cannot sit passive to watch our growth. Good or bad, straight or crooked, we must make our fate.

Nor is it ever possible or desirable that we in Canada can form an independent country. The little cry that here and there goes up among us is but the symptom of an aspiring discontent, that will not let our people longer be colonials. 'Tis but a cry forced out by what a wise man has called the growing pains of a nation's progress. Independent, we could not survive a decade. Those of us who know our country realize that beneath its surface smoulder still the embers of racial feud and of religious bitterness. Twice in our generation has the sudden alarm of conflict broken upon the quiet of our prosperity with the sound of a fire bell in the night. Not thus our path. Let us compose the feud and still the strife of races, not in the artificial partnership of an Independent Canada, but in the joint greatness of a common destiny.

Nor does our future lie in Union with those that dwell to the southward. The day of annexation to the United States is passed. Our future lies elsewhere. Be it said without concealment and without bitterness. They have chosen their lot; we have chosen ours. Let us go our separate ways in peace. Let them still keep their perennial Independence Day, with its fulminating fireworks and its Yankee Doodle. We keep our Magna Charta and our rough and ready Rule Britannia, shouting as lustily as they! The propaganda of Annexation is dead. Citizens we want, indeed, but not the prophets of an alien gospel. To you who come across our western border we can offer a land fatter than your Kansas, a government better than Montana, a climate kinder than your Dakota. Take it, Good Sir, if you will: but if, in taking it, you still raise your little croak of annexation, then up with you by the belt and out with you, breeches first, through the air, to the land of your origin! This in all friendliness.

Not independence then, not annexation, not stagnation: nor yet that doctrine of a little Canada that some conceive — half in, half out of the Empire, with a mimic navy of its own; a pretty navy this — poor two-penny collection, frollicking on its little way strictly within the Gulf of St Lawrence, a sort of silly adjunct to the navy of the Empire, semi-detached, the better to be smashed at will. As well a Navy of the Province, or the Parish, home-made for use at home, docked every Saturday in Lake Nipigon!

Yet this you say, you of the Provincial Rights, you Little Canada Man, is all we can afford! We that have raised our public charge from forty up to eighty millions odd within the ten years past, and scarce have felt the added strain of it. Nay, on the question of the cost, good gentlemen of the council, spare it not. Measure not the price. It is not a commercial benefit we buy. We are buying back our honour as Imperial Citizens. For, look you, this protection of our lives and coast, this safe-guard from the scourge of war, we have it now as much as you of England: you from the hard-earned money that you pay, we as the peasant pensioners on your Imperial Bounty.

Thus stands the case. Thus stands the question of the future of Canada. Find for us something other than mere colonial stagnation, something sounder than independence, nobler than annexation, greater in purpose than a Little Canada. Find us a way. Build us a plan, that shall make us, in hope at least, an Empire Permanent and Indivisible.

Literature and education in America

IT MAY be well to remind the reader at the outset of this article that Canada is in America. A Canadian writer may therefore with no great impropriety use the term American, for want of any other word, in reference to the literature and education of all the English-speaking people between the Rio Grande and the North Pole. There is, moreover, a certain warrant of fact for such a usage. Canadian literature — as far as there is such a thing — Canadian journalism, and the education and culture of the mass of the people of Canada approximates more nearly to the type and standard of the United States than to those of Great Britain. Whatever accusations may be brought against the literature and education of the American repub-lic apply equally well — indeed very probably apply with even greater force — to the Dominion of Canada.

This modest apology may fittingly be offered before throwing stones at the glass house in which both the Canadians and the Americans proper dwell.

Now it is a fact which had better be candidly confessed than indignantly denied that up to the present time the contribution of America to the world's great literature has been disappointingly small. There are no doubt great exceptions. We number at least some of the world's great writers on this side of the Atlantic. American humour, in reputation at any rate, may claim equality if not pre-eminence. And the signs are not wanting — they are seen in the intense realism of our short stories, and the concentrated power of our one-act plays — that we may some day come into our own. But in spite of this, the indictment holds good that up to the present we have fallen far short of what might have been properly expected of our civilisation.

I am quite aware that on this point I shall meet denial at the outset.

I once broached this question of the relative inferiority of the literary output of America to that of the old world to a gentleman from Kentucky. He answered, 'I am afraid, sir, you are imperfectly acquainted with the work of our Kentucky poets.' In the same way a friend of mine from Maryland has assured me that immediately before the war that state had witnessed the most remarkable literary development recorded since the time of Plato. I am also credibly informed that the theological essayists of Prince Edward Island challenge comparison with those of any age. It is no doubt not the fault of the Islanders that this challenge has not yet been accepted. But I am speaking here not of that literature which, though excellent in its way, is known only to the immediate locality which it adorns, but rather of those works of such eminent merit and such wide repute as to be properly classed among the literature of the world. To what a very small share of this, during the last hundred years of our history, can we in America lay claim.

This phenomenon becomes all the more remarkable when we reflect upon the unparalleled advance that has been made in this country in the growth of population, in material resources, and in the purely mechanical side of progress. Counted after the fashion of the census taker, which is our favourite American method of computation, we now number over a hundred million souls. It is some seventy years since our rising population equalled and passed that of the British Isles: a count of heads, dead and alive, during the century would show us more numerous than the British people by two to one: we erect buildings fifty stories high: we lay a mile of railroad track in twenty-four hours: the corn that we grow and the hogs that we raise are the despair of aristocratic Europe; and yet when it comes to the production of real literature, the benighted people of the British Islands can turn out more of it in a twelvemonth than our hundred million souls can manufacture in three decades.

For proof of this, if proof is needed, one has but to consider fairly and dispassionately the record of the century. How few are the names of first rank that we can offer to the world. In poetry Longfellow, Bryant, Lowell, Whittier, Whitman, with two or three others exhaust the list: of historians of the front rank we have Bancroft, Motley, Prescott, and in a liberal sense, Francis Parkman: of novelists, tale writers and essayists we can point with pride to Irving, Poe, Cooper, Hawthorne, Emerson, James, and some few others as names that are known to the world: of theologians we have Colonel Ingersoll, Mrs Eddy, and Caroline Nation. But brilliant as many of these writers are, can one for a moment compare them with the imposing list of the great names that adorn the annals of British literature in the nineteenth century? Wordsworth, Coleridge, Byron, Shelley, Keats, Tennyson, Browning, Swinburne are household names to every educated American. Novelists and tale writers such as Dickens, Thackeray, Eliot, Meredith, Kipling, and Stevenson cannot be matched in our country. How seldom are essayists and historians of the class of Carlyle, Macaulay, Gibbon, Green, Huxley, Arnold, Morley, and Bryce produced among our hundred million of free and enlightened citizens. These and a hundred other illustrious names spring to one's mind to illustrate the splendour of British literature in the nineteenth century. But surely it is unfair to ourselves to elaborate needlessly so plain a point. The candid reader will be fain to admit that the bulk of the valuable literature of the English-speaking peoples written within the last hundred years has been produced within the British Isles.

Nor can we plead in extenuation that inspiration has been lacking to us. Indeed the very contrary is the case. What can be conceived more stimulating to the poetic imagination than the advance of American civilisation into the broad plains of the Mississippi and the Saskatchewan, the passage of the unknown mountains and the descent of the treasure seekers upon the Eldorado of the coast? What finer background for literature than the silent untravelled forests and the broad rivers moving to unknown seas? In older countries the landscape is known and circumscribed. Parish church, and village, and highway succeed one another in endless alternation. There is nothing to discover, no untraversed country to penetrate. There is no mystery beyond. Thus if the old world is rich in history, rich in associations that render the simple compass of a village green a sacred spot as the battleground of long ago, so too is the new world rich in the charm and mystery of the unknown, and in the lofty stimulus that comes from the unbroken silence of the primeval forest. It was within the darkness of ancient woods that the spirits were first conceived in the imagination of mankind and that literature had its birth. A Milton or a Bunyan, that could dream dreams and see visions within the prosaic streets of an English country town — would such a man have found no inspiration could he have stood at night where the wind roars among the pine forests of the Peace, or where the cold lights of the Aurora illumine the endless desolation of the north? But alas, the Miltons and the Bunyans are not among us. The aspect of primeval nature does not call to our minds the vision of Unseen Powers riding upon the midnight blast. To us the midnight blast represents an enormous quantity of horse-power going to waste; the primeval forest is a first-class site for a saw mill, and the leaping cataract tempts us to erect a red-brick hydro-electric establishment on its banks and make it leap to some purpose.

The fact of the matter is that despite our appalling numerical growth and mechanical progress, despite the admirable physical appliances offered by our fountain pens, our pulp-wood paper, and our linotype machine, the progress of literature and the general diffusion of literary appreciation on this continent is not commensurate with the other aspects of our social growth. Our ordinary citizen in America is not a literary person. He has but little instinct towards letters, a very restricted estimation of literature as an art, and neither envy nor admiration for those who cultivate it. A book for him means a thing by which the strain on the head is relieved after the serious business of the day and belongs in the same general category as a burlesque show or a concertina solo: general information means a general knowledge of the results of the last election, and philosophical speculation is represented by speculation upon the future of the Democratic party. Education is synonymous with ability to understand the stock-exchange page of the morning paper, and culture means a silk hat and the habit of sleeping in pyjamas.

Not the least striking feature in the literary sterility of America is the fact that we are, at any rate as measured by any mechanical standard, a very highly educated people. If education can beget literature, it is here in America that the art of letters should most chiefly flourish. In no country in the world is more time, more thought, and more money spent upon education than in America. School books pour from our presses in tons. Manuals are prepared by the million, for use either with or without a teacher, manuals for the deaf, manuals for the dumb, manuals for the deficient, for the half-deficient, for the three-quarters deficient, manuals of hygiene for the feeble and manuals of temperance for the drunk. Instruction can be had orally, vocally, verbally, by correspondence or by mental treatment. Twelve million of our children are at school. The most skilful examiners apply to them every examination that human cruelty can invent or human fortitude can endure. In higher education alone thirty-five thousand professors lecture unceasingly to three hundred thousand students. Surely so vast and complicated a machine might be expected to turn out scholars, poets, and men of letters such as the world has never seen before. Yet it is surprising that the same unliterary, anti-literary tendency that is seen throughout our whole social environment, manifests itself also in the peculiar and distorted form given in our higher education and in the singular barrenness of its results.

There can be no greater contrast than that offered by the system of education in Great Britain, broad and almost planless in its outline, yet admirable in its results and the carefully planned and organised higher education of America. The one, in some indefinable way, fosters, promotes, and develops the true instinct of literature. It puts a premium upon genius. It singles out originality and mental power and accentuates natural inequality, caring less for the commonplace achievements of the many than for the transcendent merit of the few. The other system absurdly attempts to reduce the whole range of higher attainment to the measured and organised grinding of a mill: it undertakes to classify ability and to measure intellectual progress with a yard measure, and to turn out in its graduates a 'standardised' article similar to steel rails or structural beams, with interchangeable parts in their brains and all of them purchasable in the market at the standard price.

The root of the matter and its essential bearing upon the question of literary development in general is that the two systems of education take their start from two entirely opposite points of view.

The older view of education, which is rapidly passing away in America, but which is still dominant in the great universities of England, aimed at a wide and humane culture of the intellect. It regarded the various departments of learning as forming essentially a unity, some pursuit of each being necessary to the intelligent comprehension of the whole, and a reasonable grasp of the whole being necessary to the appreciation of each. It is true that the system followed in endeavouring to realise this ideal took as its basis the literature of Greece and Rome. But this was rather made the starting point for a general knowledge of the literature, the history and the philosophy of all ages than regarded as offering in itself the final goal of education.

Now our American system pursues a different path. It breaks up the field of knowledge into many departments, subdivides these into special branches and sections, and calls upon the scholar to devote himself to microscopic activity in some part of a section of a branch of a department of the general field of learning. This specialised system of education that we pursue does not of course begin at once. Any system of training must naturally first devote itself to the acquiring of a rudimentary knowledge of such elementary things as reading, spelling, and the humbler aspects of mathematics. But the further the American student proceeds the more this tendency to specialisation asserts itself. When he enters upon what are called post-graduate studies, he is expected to become altogether a specialist, devoting his whole mind to the study of the left foot of the garden frog, or to the use of the ablative in Tacitus, or to the history of the first half hour of the Reformation. As he continues on his upward way, the air about him gets rarer and rarer, his path becomes more and more solitary until he reaches, and encamps upon, his own little pinnacle of refined knowledge staring at his feet and ignorant of the world about him, the past behind him, and the future before him. At the end of his labours he publishes a useless little pamphlet called his thesis which is new in the sense that nobody ever wrote it before, and erudite in the sense that nobody will ever read it. Meantime the American student's ignorance of all things except his own part of his own subject has grown colossal. The unused parts of his intellect have ossified. His interest in general literature, his power of original thought, indeed his wish to think at all, is far less than it was in the second year of his undergraduate course. More than all that, his interestingness to other people has completely departed. Even with his fellow scholars so-called he can find no common ground of intellectual intercourse. If three men sit down together and one is a philologist, the second a numismatist, and the third a subsection of a conchologist, what can they find to talk about?

I have had occasion in various capacities to see something of the working of this system of the higher learning. Some years ago I resided for a month or two with a group of men who were specialists of the type described, most of them in pursuit of their degree of Doctor of Philosophy, some of them — easily distinguished by their air of complete vacuity — already in possession of it. The first night I dined with them, I addressed to the man opposite me some harmless question about a recent book that I thought of general interest. 'I don't know anything about that,' he answered, 'I'm in sociology.' There was nothing to do but to beg his pardon and to apologise for not having noticed it.

Another of these same men was studying classics on the same plan. He was engaged in composing a doctor's thesis on the genitive of value in Plautus. For eighteen months past he had read nothing but Plautus. The manner of his reading was as follows: first he read Plautus all through and picked out all the verbs of estimating followed by the genitive, then he read it again and picked out the verbs of reckoning, then the verbs of wishing, praying, cursing, and so on. Of all these he made lists and grouped them into little things called Tables of Relative Frequency, which, when completed, were about as interesting, about as useful, and about as easy to compile as the list of wholesale prices of sugar at New Orleans. Yet this man's thesis was admittedly the best in his year, and it was considered by his instructors that had he not died immediately after graduation, he would have lived to publish some of the most daring speculations on the genitive of value in Plautus that the world has ever seen.

I do not here mean to imply that all our scholars of this type die, or even that they ought to die, immediately after graduation. Many of them remain alive for years, though their utility has of course largely departed after their thesis is complete. Still they do and can remain alive. If kept in a dry atmosphère and not exposed to the light, they may remain in an almost perfect state of preservation for years after finishing their doctor's thesis. I remember once seeing a specimen of this kind enter into a country post-office store, get his letters, and make a few purchases, closely scrutinised by the rural occupants. When he had gone out the postmaster turned to a friend with the triumphant air of a man who has information in reserve and said, 'Now wouldn't you think, to look at him, that man was a d_d fool?' 'Certainly would,' said the friend, slowly nodding his head. 'Well, he isn't,' said the postmaster emphatically; 'he's a Doctor of Philosophy.' But the distinction was too subtle for most of the auditors.

In passing these strictures upon our American system of higher education, I do not wish to be misunderstood. One must of course admit a certain amount of specialisation in study. It is quite reasonable that a young man with a particular aptitude or inclination towards modern languages, or classical literature, or political economy, should devote himself particularly to that field. But what I protest against is the idea that each of these studies is apt with us to be regarded as wholly exclusive of the others, and that the moment a man becomes a student of German literature he should lose all interest in general history and philosophy, and be content to remain as ignorant of political economy or jurisprudence as a plumber. The price of liberty, it has been finely said, is eternal vigilance, and I think one may say that the price of real intellectual progress is eternal alertness, an increasing and growing interest in all great branches of human knowledge. Art is notoriously long and life is infamously short. We cannot know everything. But we can at least pursue the ideal of knowing the greatest things in all branches of knowledge, something at least of the great masters of literature, something of the best of the world's philosophy, and something of its political conduct and structure. It is but little that the student can ever know, but we can at least see that the little is wisely distributed.

And here perhaps it is necessary to make a further qualification to this antagonism of the principle of specialisation. I quite admit its force and purpose as applied to such things as natural science and medicine. These are branches capable of isolation from the humanities in general, and in them progress is not dependent on the width of general culture. Here it is necessary that a certain portion of the learned world should isolate themselves from mankind, immure themselves in laboratories, testing, dissecting, weighing, probing, boiling, mixing, and cooking to their heart's content. It is necessary for the world's work that they should do so. In any case this is real research work done by real specialists *after* their education and not *as* their education. Of this work the so-called researches of the graduate student, who spends three years in writing a thesis on John Milton's god-mother, is a mere parody.

Nor is it to be thought that this post-graduate work upon the preparation of a thesis, this so-called original scholarship is difficult. It is pretentious, plausible, esoteric, cryptographic, occult, if you will, but difficult it is not. It is of course laborious. It takes time. But the amount of intellect called for in the majority of these elaborate compilations is about the same, or rather less, than that involved in posting the day book in a village grocery. The larger part of it is on a level with the ordinary routine clerical duties performed by a young lady stenographer for ten dollars a week. One must also quite readily admit that just as there is false and real research, so too is there such a thing as a false and make-believe general education. Education, I allow, can be made so broad that it gets thin, so extensive that it must be shallow. The educated mind of this type becomes so wide that it appears quite flat. Such is the education of the drawing-room conversationalist. Thus a man may acquire no little reputation as a classical scholar by constant and casual reference to Plato or Diodorus Siculus without in reality having studied anything more arduous than the Home Study Circle of his weekly paper. Yet even such a man, pitiable though he is, may perhaps be viewed with a more indulgent eye than the ossified specialist.

It is of course not to be denied that there is even in the field of the humanities a certain amount of investigation to be done – of research work, if one will – of a highly specialised character. But this is work that can best be done not by way of an educational training – for its effect is usually the reverse of educational, but as a special labour performed for its own sake as the life work of a trained scholar, not as the examination requirement of a prospective candidate. The pretentious claim made by so many of our universities that the thesis presented for the doctor's degree must represent a distinct contribution to human knowledge will not stand examination. Distinct contributions to human knowledge are not so easily nor so mechanically achieved. Nor should it be thought either that, even where an elaborate and painstaking piece of research has been carried on by a trained scholar, such an achievement should carry with it any recognition of a very high order. It is useful and meritorious no doubt, but the esteem in which it is held in the academic world in America indicates an entirely distorted point of view. Our American process of research has led to an absurd admiration of the mere collection of facts, extremely useful things in their way but in point of literary eminence standing in the same class as the Twelfth Census of the United States or the Statistical Abstract of the United Kingdom. So it has come to pass that the bulk of our college-made books are little more than collections of material out of which in the hands of a properly gifted person a book might be made. In our book-making in America – our serious book-making, I mean – the whole art of presentation, the thing that ought to be the very essence of literature, is sadly neglected. 'A fact,' as Lord Bryce once said in addressing the assembled historians of America, 'is an excellent thing and you must have facts to write about; but you should realise that even a fact before it is ready for presentation must be cut and polished like a diamond.' 'You need not be afraid to be flippant,' said the same eminent authority, 'but you ought to have a horror of being dull.' Unfortunately our American college-bred authors cannot be flippant if they try: it is at best but the lumbering playfulness of the elephant, humping his heavy posteriors in the air and wiggling his little tail in the vain attempt to be a lamb.

The head and front of the indictment thus presented against American scholarship is seen in its results. It is not making scholars in the highest sense of the term. It is not encouraging a true culture. It is not aiding in the creation of a real literature. The whole bias of it is contrary to the development of the highest intellectual power: it sets a man of genius to a drudging task suitable to the capacities of third-class clerk, substitutes the machine-made pedant for the man of letters, puts a premium on painstaking dullness and breaks down genius, inspiration, and originality in the grinding routine of the college tread-mill. Here and there, as is only natural, conspicuous exceptions appear in the academic world of America. A New England professor has invested the dry subject of government with a charm that is only equalled by the masterly comprehensiveness of his treatment: a Massachusetts philosopher held for a lifetime the ear of the educated world, and an American professor has proved that even so abstruse a subject as the history of political philosophy can be presented in a form at once powerful and fascinating.

But even the existence of these brilliant exceptions to the general rule cannot invalidate the proposition that the effect of our American method upon the cycle of higher studies is depressing in the extreme. History is dwindling into fact lore and is becoming the science of the almanac; economics is being buried alive in statistics and is degenerating into the science of the census; literature is stifled by philology, and is little better than the science of the lexicographer.

Nor is it only in the higher ranges of education and book-making that the same abiding absence of general literary spirit is manifest in American life. For below, or at least parallel with the universities we have the equally notable case of our American newspapers and journals. In nearly all of these the art of writing is relegated entirely to the background. Our American newspapers and journals (with certain notable and honourable exceptions) are not written 'upwards' (so to speak) as if seeking to attain the ideal of an elevated literary excellence, but 'downward,' so as to catch the ear and capture the money of the crowd. Here obtrudes himself the everlasting American man with the dinner pail, admirable as a political and industrial institution but despicable as the touch-stone of a national literature. Our newspapers must be written down to his level. Our poetry must be put in a form that he can understand. Our sonnets must be tuned to suit his ear. Our editorials must speak his own tongue. Otherwise he will not spend his magical one cent and our newspaper cannot circulate. Hence it is that the bulk of our current journalistic literature is strictly a one-cent literature. This is the situation that has evolved that weird being called the American Reporter, tireless in his activity, omnipresent, omnivorous, and omni-ignorant. He is out looking for facts, but of the art of presenting them with either accuracy or attraction he is completely innocent. He has just enough knowledge of shorthand to be able completely to mystify himself; and in deciphering his notes of events, speeches, and occurrences, to fall back upon his general education would be like falling back upon a cucumber frame.

I cannot do better to illustrate the amount of literary power possessed by the American reporter than to take an actual illustration or at any rate one that is as good as actual. I will take a selection from President Lincoln's Second Inaugural Address and will present it first as Lincoln is known to have written it, and secondly as the Washington reporters of the day are certain to have reported it. Here is the original: 'Fondly do we hope, fervently do we pray, that this mighty scourge of war may soon pass away. Yet if God wills that it continue until all the wealth piled by the bondsman's two hundred and fifty years of unrequited toil shall be sunk, and until every drop of blood drawn with the lash shall be paid with another drawn with the sword; as was said three thousand years ago, so still it must be said, "the judgments of the Lord are true and righteous altogether." '

Here is the reproduction of the above at the hands of the American reporter, piecing out his meagre knowledge of stenography by the use of his still more meagre literary ability: 'Mr Lincoln then spoke at some length upon the general subject of prayer. He said that prayer was fond and foolish, but that war would scourge it out. War was a nightly scourge. It would pile up two hundred and fifty million dollars of unpaid bonds. He recommended the lash as the most appropriate penalty, and concluded by expressing his opinion that the judgments of the Lord were altogether ridiculous.'

The ultimate psychology of this decided absence of literary power in our general intellectual development would be difficult to appreciate. It may be that the methods adopted in our education are a consequence rather than a cause, and it may well be also that, even if our educative system is a contributory factor, other causes of great potency are operative at the same time. One of these no doubt is found in the distinct bias of our whole American life towards commercialism. The vastly greater number of us in America have always been under the shameful necessity of earning our own living. This has coloured all our thinking with the yellow tinge of the dollar. Social and intellectual values necessarily undergo a peculiar readjustment among a people to whom individually the 'main chance' is necessarily everything. Thus it is that with us everything tends to find itself 'upon a business basis.' Organisation and business methods are obtruded everywhere. Public enthusiasm is replaced by the manufactured hysteria of the convention. The old-time college president, such as the one of Harvard who lifted up his voice in prayer in the twilight of a summer evening over the 'rebels' that were to move on Bunker Hill that night, is replaced by the Modern Business President, alert and brutal in his methods, and himself living only on sufferance after the age of forty years. A good clergyman with us must be a hustler. The only missionary we care for is an advertiser, and even the undertaker must send us a Christmas calendar if he desires to retain our custom. Everything with us is 'run' on business lines from a primary election to a prayer meeting. Thus business, and the business code, and business principles become everything. Smartness is the quality most desired, pecuniary success the goal to be achieved. Hence all less tangible and provable forms of human merit, and less tangible aspirations of the human mind are rudely shouldered aside by business ability and commercial success. There follows the apotheosis of the business man. He is elevated to the post of national hero. His most stupid utterances are taken down by the American Reporter, through the prism of whose intellect they are refracted with a double brilliance and inscribed at large in the pages of the one-cent press. The man who organises a soap-and-glue company is called a nation builder; a person who can borrow enough money to launch a Distiller's Association is named an empire maker, and a man who remains in business until he is seventy-five without getting into the penitentiary is designated a Grand Old Man.

But it may well be that there is a reason for our literary inferiority lying deeper still than the commercial environment and the existence of an erroneous educational ideal, which are but things of the surface. It is possible that after all literature and progress-happiness-and-equality are antithetical terms. Certain it is that the world's greatest literature has arisen in the darkest hours of its history. More than one of the masterpieces of the past were written in a dungeon. It is perhaps conceivable that literature has arisen in the past mainly on the basis of the inequalities, the sufferings and the misery of the common lot that has led humanity to seek in the concepts of the imagination the happiness that seemed denied by the stern environment of reality. Thus perhaps American civilisation with its public school and the dead level of its elementary instruction, with its simple code of republicanism and its ignorance of the glamour and mystery of monarchy, with its bread and work for all and its universal hope of the betterment of personal fortune, contains in itself an atmosphere in which the flower of literature cannot live. It is at least conceivable that this flower blossoms most beautifully in the dark places of the world, among that complex of tyranny and heroism, of inexplicable cruelty and sublime suffering that is called history. Perhaps this literary sterility of America is but the mark of the new era that is to come not to America alone, but to the whole of our western civilisation; the era in which humanity, fed to satiety and housed and warmed to the point of somnolence, with its wars abolished and its cares removed, may find that it has lost from among it that supreme gift of literary inspiration which was the comforter of its darker ages.

The apology of a professor:

An essay on modern learning

I KNOW no more interesting subject of speculation, nor any more calculated to allow of a fair-minded difference of opinion, than the enquiry whether a professor has any right to exist. *Prima facie,* of course, the case is heavily against him. His angular overcoat, his missing buttons, and his faded hat, will not bear comparison with the double-breasted splendour of the stock broker, or the *Directoire* fur gown of the cigar maker. Nor does a native agility of body compensate for the missing allurement of dress. He cannot skate. He does not shoot. He must not swear. He is not brave. His mind, too, to the outsider at any rate, appears defective and seriously damaged by education. He cannot appreciate a twenty-five-cent novel, or a melodrama, or a moving-picture show, or any of that broad current of intellectual movement which soothes the brain of the business man in its moments of inactivity. His conversation, even to the tolerant, is impossible. Apparently he has neither ideas nor enthusiasms, nothing but an elaborate catalogue of dead men's opinions which he cites with a petulant and peevish authority that will not brook contradiction, and that must be soothed by a tolerating acquiescence, or flattered by a plenary acknowledgment of ignorance.

Yet the very heaviness of this initial indictment against the professor might well suggest to an impartial critic that there must at least be mitigating circumstances in the case. Even if we are to admit that the indictment is well founded, the reason is all the greater for examining the basis on which it rests. At any rate some explanation of the facts involved may perhaps serve to palliate, if not to remove, demerits which are rather to be deplored than censured. It is one of the standing defects of our age that social classes, or let us say more narrowly, social categories, know so little of one another. For the purposes of ready reckoning, of that handy transaction of business which is the passion of the hour, we have adopted a way of labelling one another with the tag mark of a profession or an occupation that becomes an aid to business but a barrier to intercourse. This man is a professor, that man an 'insurance man,' a third – *terque quaterque beatus* – a 'liquor man'; with these are 'railroad men,' 'newspaper men,' 'dry goods men,' and so forth. The things that we handle for our livelihood impose themselves upon our personality, till the very word 'man' drops out, and a gentleman is referred to as a 'heavy pulp and paper interest' while another man is a prominent 'rubber plant,' two or three men round a dinner table become an 'iron and steel circle,' and thus it is that for the simple conception of a human being is substituted a complex of 'interests,' 'rings,' 'circles,' 'sets,' and other semi-geometrical figures arising out of avocations rather than affinities. Hence it comes that insurance men mingle with insurance men, liquor men mix, if one may use the term without afterthought, with liquor men: what looks like a lunch between three men at a club is really a cigar having lunch with a couple of plugs of tobacco.

Now the professor more than any ordinary person finds himself shut out from the general society of the business world. The rest of the 'interests' have, after all, some things in common. The circles intersect at various points. Iron and steel has a certain fellowship with pulp and paper, and the whole lot of them may be converted into the common ground of preference shares and common stock. But the professor is to all of them an outsider. Hence his natural dissimilarity is unduly heightened in its appearance by the sort of avocational isolation in which he lives.

Let us look further into the status and the setting of the man. To begin with, history has been hard upon him. For some reason the strenuous men of activity and success in the drama of life have felt an instinctive scorn of the academic class, which they have been at no pains to conceal. Bismarck knew of no more bitter taunt to throw at the Free Trade economists of England than to say that they were all either clergymen or professors. Napoleon felt a life-long abhorrence of the class, broken only by one brief experiment that ended in failure. It is related that at the apogee of the Imperial rule, the idea flashed upon him that France must have learned men, that the professors must be encouraged. He decided to act at once. Sixty-five professors were invited that evening to the palace of the Tuileries. They came. They stood about in groups, melancholy and myopic beneath the light. Napoleon spoke to them in turn. To the first he spoke of fortifications. The professor in reply referred to the binomial theorem. 'Put him out,' said Napoleon. To the second he spoke of commerce. The professor in answer cited the opinions of Diodorus Siculus. 'Put him out,' said Napoleon. At the end of half an hour Napoleon had had enough of the professors. 'Cursed idealogues,' he cried; 'put them all out.' Nor were they ever again admitted.

Nor is it only in this way that the course of history has been unkind to the professor. It is a notable fact in the past, that all persons of eminence who might have shed a lustre upon the academic class are absolved from the title of professor, and the world at large is ignorant that they ever wore it. We never hear of the author of *The Wealth of Nations* as Professor Smith, nor do we know the poet of *Evangeline* as Professor Longfellow. The military world would smile to see the heroes of the Southern Confederacy styled Professor Lee and Professor Jackson. We do not know of Professor Harrison as the occupant of a President's chair. Those whose talk is of dreadnoughts and of strategy never speak of Professor Mahan, and France has long since forgotten the proper title of Professor Guizot and Professor Taine. Thus it is that the ingratitude of an undiscerning public robs the professorial class of the honour of its noblest names. Nor does the evil stop there. For, in these latter days at least, the same public which eliminates the upward range of the term, applies it downwards and sideways with indiscriminating generality. It is a 'professor' who plays upon the banjo. A 'professor' teaches swimming. Hair cutting, as an art, is imparted in New York by 'professors'; while any gentleman whose thaumaturgic intercommunication with the world of spirits has reached the point of interest which warrants space advertising in the daily press, explains himself as a 'professor' to his prospective clients. So it comes that the true professor finds all his poor little attributes of distinction – his mock dignity, his gown, his string of supplementary letters – all taken over by a mercenary age to be exploited, as the stock in trade of an up-to-date advertiser. The vendor of patent medicine depicts himself in the advertising columns in a gown, with an uplifted hand to shew the Grecian draping of the fold. After his name are placed enough letters and full stops to make up a simultaneous equation in algebra.

The word 'professor' has thus become a generic term, indicating the assumption of any form of dexterity, from hair-cutting to running the steam shovel in a crematorium. It is even customary – I am informed – to designate in certain haunts of meretricious gaiety the gentleman whose efforts at the piano are rewarded by a *per capita* contribution of ten cents from every guest – the 'professor.'

One may begin to see, perhaps, the peculiar disadvantage under which the professor labours in finding his avocation confused with the various branches of activity for which he can feel nothing but a despairing admiration. But there are various ways also in which the very circumstances of his profession cramp and bind him. In the first place there is no doubt that his mind is very seriously damaged by his perpetual contact with the students. I would not for a moment imply that a university would be better off without the students; although the point is one which might well elicit earnest discussion. But their effect upon the professor is undoubtedly bad. He is surrounded by an atmosphere of sycophantic respect. His students, on his morning arrival, remove his overshoes and hang up his overcoat. They sit all day writing down his lightest words with stylographic pens of the very latest model. They laugh at the meanest of his jests. They treat him with a finely simulated respect that has come down as a faint tradition of the old days of Padua and Bologna, when a professor was in reality the venerated master, a man who wanted to teach, and the students disciples who wanted to learn.

All that is changed now. The supreme import of the professor to the students now lies in the fact that he controls the examinations. He holds the golden key which will unlock the door of the temple of learning — unlock it, that is, not to let the student in, but to let him get out — into something decent. This fact gives to the professor a fictitious importance, easily confounded with his personality, similar to that of the gate keeper at a dog show, or the ticket wicket man at a hockey match.

In this is seen some part of the consequences of the vast, organised thing called modern education. Everything has the merits of its defects. It is a grand thing and a possible thing, that practically all people should possess the intellectual-mechanical arts of reading, writing, and computation: good too that they should possess pigeonholed and classified data of the geography and history of the world; admirable too that they should possess such knowledge of the principles of natural science as will enable them to put a washer on a kitchen tap, or inflate a motor tire with a soda-syphon bottle. All this is splendid. This we have got. And this places us collectively miles above the rude illiterate men of arms, burghers, and villeins of the middle ages who thought the moon took its light from God, whereas we know that its light is simply a function of π divided by the square of its distance.

Let me not get confused in my thesis. I am saying that the universal distribution of mechanical education is a fine thing, and that we have also proved it possible. But above this is the utterly different thing — we have no good word for it, call it learning, wisdom, enlightenment, anything you will — which means not a mechanical acquirement from without but something done from within: a power and willingness to think: an interest, for its own sake, in that general enquiry into the form and meaning of life which constitutes the ground plan of education. Now this, desirable though it is, cannot be produced by the mechanical compulsion of organised education. It belongs, and always has, to the few and never to the many. The ability to think is rare. Any man can think and think hard when he has to: the savage devotes a nicety of thought to the equipoise of his club, or the business man to the adjustment of a market price. But the ability or desire to think without compulsion about things that neither warm the hands nor fill the stomach, is very rare. Reflexion on the riddle of life, the cruelty of death, the innate savagery and the sublimity of the creature man, the history and progress of man in his little earth-dish of trees and flowers — all these things taken either 'straight' in the masculine form of philosophy and the social sciences, or taken by diffusion through the feminised form literature, constitute the operation of the educated mind. Of all these things most people in their degree think a little and then stop. They realise presently that these things are very difficult, and that they don't matter, and that there is no money in them. Old men never think of them at all. They are glad enough to stay in the warm daylight a little longer. For a working solution of these problems different things are done. Some people use a clergyman. Others declare that the Hindoos know all about it. Others, especially of late, pay a reasonable sum for the services of a professional thaumaturgist who supplies a solution of the soul problem by mental treatment at long range, radiating from State St, Chicago. Others, finally, of a native vanity that will not admit itself vanquished, buckle about themselves a few little formulas of 'evolution' and 'force,' co-relate the conception of God to the differentiation of a frog's foot, and strut through life emplumed with the rump-feathers of their own conceit.

I trust my readers will not think that I have forgotten my professor. I have not. All of this digression is but an instance of *reculer pour mieux sauter.* It is necessary to bring out all this back-ground of the subject to show the setting in which the professor is placed.

Possibly we shall begin to see that behind this quaint being in his angular overcoat are certain greater facts in respect to the general relation of education to the world of which the professor is only a product, and which help to explain, if they do not remove, the dislocated misfit of his status among his fellow men. We were saying then that the truly higher education – thought about life, mankind, literature, art – cannot be handed out at will. To attempt to measure it off by the yard, to mark it out into stages and courses, to sell it at the commutation rate represented by a college sessional fee – all this produces a contradiction in terms. For the thing itself is substituted an imitation of it. For real wisdom – obtainable only by the few – is substituted a nickel-plated make-believe obtainable by any person of ordinary intellect who has the money, and who has also, in the good old Latin sense, the needful assiduity. I am not saying that the system is bad. It is the best we can get; and incidentally, and at back-rounds it turns out a by-product in the shape of a capable and well-trained man who has forgotten all about the immortality of the soul, in which he never had any interest any way, but who conducts a law business with admirable efficiency.

The result, then, of this odd-looking system is, that what ought to be a thing existing for itself is turned into a qualification for something else. The reality of a student's studies is knocked out by the grim earnestness of having to pass an examination. How can a man really think of literature, or of the problem of the soul, who knows that he must learn the contents of a set of books in order to pass an examination which will give him the means of his own support and, perhaps, one half the support of his mother, or fifteen per cent of that of a maiden aunt. The pressure of circumstances is too much. The meaning of study is lost. The qualification is everything.

Not that the student finds his burden heavy or the situation galling. He takes the situation as he finds it, is hugely benefited by it at back-rounds, and, being young, adapts himself to it: accepts with indifference whatever programme may be needful for the qualification that he wants: studies Hebrew or Choctaw with equal readiness; and, as his education progresses, will write you a morning essay on transcendental utilitarianism, and be back again to lunch. At the end of his course he has learned much. He has learned to sit – that first requisite for high professional work – and he can sit for hours. He can write for hours with a stylographic pen: more than that, for I wish to state the case fairly, he can make a digest, or a summary, or a reproduction of anything in the world. Incidentally the *speculation* is all knocked sideways out of him. But the lack of it is never felt.

Observe that it was not so in Padua. The student came thither from afar off, on foot or on a mule; so I picture him at least in my ignorance of Italian history, seated droopingly upon a mule, with earnest, brown eyes hungered with the desire to know, and in his hand a vellum-bound copy of Thomas Aquinas written in long hand, priceless, as *he* thinks, for the wisdom it contains. Now the Padua student wanted to know: not for a qualification, not because he wanted to be a pharmaceutical expert with a municipal licence, but because he thought the things in Thomas Aquinas and such to be things of tremendous import. They were not; but he thought so. This student thought that he could really find out things: that if he listened daily to the words of the master who taught him, and read hard, and thought hard, he would presently discover real truths — the only things in life that he cared for — such as whether the soul is a fluid or a solid, whether his mule existed or was only a vapour, and much other of this sort. These things he fully expected to learn. For their sake he brought to bear on the person of his teacher that reverential admiration which survives faintly to-day, like a biological 'vestige,' in the attitude of the college student who holds the over-coat of his professor. The Padua student, too, got what he came for. After a time he knew all about the soul, all about his mule — knew, too, something of the more occult, the almost devilish sciences, perilous to tackle, such as why the sun is suspended from falling into the ocean, or the very demonology of symbolism — the AL-GEB of the Arabians — by which X + Y taken to the double or square can be shown after many days' computation to be equal to $x^2 + 2xy + y^2$.

A man with such knowledge simply *had* to teach it. What to him if he should wear a brown gown of frieze and feed on pulse! This, as beside the bursting force of the expanding steam of his knowledge, counted for nothing. So he went forth, and he in turn became a professor, a man of profound acquirement, whose control over malign comets elicited a shuddering admiration.

These last reflections seem to suggest that it is not merely that something has gone wrong with the attitude of the student and the professor towards knowledge, but that something has gone wrong with knowledge itself. We have got the thing into such a shape that we do not know one-tenth as much as we used to. Our modern scholarship has poked and pried in so many directions, has set itself to be so ultra-rational, so hyper-sceptical, that now it knows nothing at all. All the old certainty has vanished. The good old solid dogmatic dead-sureness that buckled itself in the oak and brass of its own stupidity is clean gone. It died at about the era of the country squire, the fox-hunting parson, the three-bottle Prime Minister, and the voluminous Doctor of Divinity in broadcloth imperturbable even in sobriety, and positively omniscient when drunk. We have argued them off the stage of a world all too ungrateful. In place of their sturdy outlines appear that sickly anaemic Modern Scholarship, the double-jointed jack-in-the-box, Modern Religion, the feminine angularity of Modern Morality, bearing a jug of filtered water, and behind them, as the very lord of wisdom, the grinning mechanic, Practical Science, using the broadcloth suit of the defunct doctor as his engine-room over-alls. Or if we prefer to place the same facts without the aid of personification, our learning has so watered itself down that the starch and consistency is all out of it. There is no absolute sureness anywhere. Everything is henceforth to be a development, an evolution; morals and ethics are turned from fixed facts to shifting standards that change from age to age like the fashion of our clothes; art and literature are only a product, not good or bad, but a part of its age and environment. So it comes that our formal studies are no longer a burning quest for absolute truth. We have long since discovered that we cannot know anything. Our studies consist only in the long-drawn proof of the futility for the search after knowledge effected by exposing the errors of the past. Philosophy is the science which proves that we can know nothing of the soul. Medicine is the science which tells that we know nothing of the body. Political Economy is that which teaches that we know nothing of the laws of wealth; and Theology the critical history of those errors from which we deduce our ignorance of God.

When I sit and warm my hands, as best I may, at the little heap of embers that is now Political Economy, I cannot but contrast its dying glow with the generous blaze of the vainglorious and triumphant science that once it was.

Such is the distinctive character of modern learning, imprint with a resigned agnosticism towards the search after truth, able to refute everything and to believe nothing, and leaving its once earnest devotees stranded upon the arid sands of their own ignorance. In the face of this fact can it be wondered that a university converts itself into a sort of mill, grinding out its graduates, legally qualified, with conscientious regularity? The students take the mill as they find it, perform their task and receive their reward. They listen to their professor. They write down with stylographic pens in loose-leaf note books his most inane and his most profound speculations with an undiscriminating impartiality. The reality of the subject leaves but little trace upon their minds.

All of what has been said above has been directed mainly towards the hardship of the professor's lot upon its scholastic side. Let me turn to another aspect of his life, the moral. By a strange confusion of thought a professor is presumed to be a good man. His standing association with the young and the history of his profession, which was once amalgamated with that of the priesthood, give him a connexion at one remove with morality. He therefore finds himself in that category of men – including himself and the curate as its chief representatives – to whom the world at large insists on ascribing a rectitude of character and a simplicity of speech that unfits them for ordinary society. It is gratuitously presumed that such men prefer tea to whiskey-and-soda, blindman's buff to draw poker, and a freshmen's picnic to a prize fight.

For the curate of course I hold no brief. Let him sink. In any case he has to console him the favour of the sex, a concomitant perhaps of his very harmlessness, but productive at the same time of creature comforts. Soft slippers deck his little feet, flowers lie upon his study table, and round his lungs the warmth of an embroidered chest-protector proclaims the favour of the fair. Of this the ill-starred professor shares nothing. It is a sad fact that he is at once harmless and despised. He may lecture for twenty years and never find so much as a mullein stalk upon his desk. For him no canvas slippers, knitted by fair fingers, nor the flowered gown, nor clock-worked hosiery of the ecclesiastic. The sex will have none of him. I do not mean, of course, that there are no women that form exceptions to this rule. We have all seen immolated upon the academic hearth, and married to professors, women whose beauty and accomplishments would have adorned the home of a wholesale liquor merchant. But the broad rule still obtains. Women who embody, so St Augustine has told us, the very principle of evil, can only really feel attracted towards bad men. The professor is too good for them.

Whether a professor is of necessity a good man, is a subject upon which I must not presume to dogmatise. The women may be right in voting him a 'muff.' But if he is such in any degree, the conventional restrictions of his profession tend to heighten it. The bursts of profanity that are hailed as a mark of business energy on the part of a railroad magnate or a cabinet minister are interdicted to a professor. It is a canon of his profession that he must never become violent, nor lift his hand in anger. I believe that it was not always so. The story runs, authentic enough, that three generations ago a Harvard professor in a fit of anger with a colleague (engendered, if I recall the case, by the discussion of a nice point in thermo-dynamics) threw him into a chemical furnace and burned him. But the buoyancy of those days is past. In spite of the existence of our up-to-date apparatus, I do not believe that any of our present professoriate has yielded to such an impulse.

One other point remains worthy of remark in the summation of the heavy disadvantages under which the professor lives and labours. He does not know how to make money. This is a grave fault, and one that in the circumstances of the day can scarcely be overlooked. It comes down to him as a legacy of the Padua days when the professor neither needed money nor thought of it. Now when he would like money he is hampered by an 'evoluted' inability to get hold of it. He dares not commercialise his profession, or does not know how to do so. Had he the business instinct of the leaders of labour and the master manufacturers, he would long since have set to work at the problem. He would have urged his government to put so heavy a tax on the import of foreign professors as to keep the home market for himself. He would have organised himself into amalgamated Brotherhoods of Instructors of Latin, United Greek Workers of America, and so forth, organised strikes, picketed the houses of the college trustees, and made himself a respected place as a member of industrial society. This his inherited inaptitude forbids him to do.

Nor can the professor make money out of what he knows. Somehow a plague is on the man. A teacher of English cannot write a half-dime novel, nor a professor of dynamics invent a safety razor. The truth is that a modern professor for commercial purposes doesn't know anything. He only knows parts of things.

It occurred to me some years ago when the Cobalt silver mines were first discovered that a professor of scientific attainments ought to be able, by transferring his talent to that region, to amass an enormous fortune. I questioned one of the most gifted of my colleagues. 'Could you not,' I asked, 'as a specialist in metals discover silver mines at sight?' 'Oh, no,' he said, shuddering at the very idea, 'you see I'm not a metallurgist; at Cobalt the silver is all in the rocks and I know nothing of rocks whatever.' 'Who then,' I said, 'knows about rocks?' 'For that,' he answered, 'you need a geologist like Adamson; but then, you see, he knows the rocks, but doesn't know the silver.' 'But could you not both go,' I said, 'and Adamson hold the rock while you extracted the silver?' 'Oh, no,' the professor answered, 'you see we are neither of us mining engineers; and even then we ought to have a good hydraulic man and an electric man.' 'I suppose,' I said, 'that if I took about seventeen of you up there you might find something. No? Well, would it not be possible to get somebody who would know something of *all* these things?' 'Yes,' he said, 'any of the fourth-year students would, but personally all that I do is to reduce the silver when I get it.' 'That I can do myself,' I answered musingly, and left him.

Such then is the professor; a man whose avocation in life is hampered by the history of its past: imparting in the form of statutory exercises knowledge that in its origin meant a spontaneous effort of the intelligence, whose very learning itself has become a profession rather than a pursuit, whose mock dignity and fictitious morality remove him from the society of his own sex and deny to him the favour of the other. Surely, in this case, to understand is to sympathise. Is it not possible, too, that when all is said and done the professor is performing a useful service in the world, unconsciously of course, in acting as a leaven in the lump of commercialism that sits so heavily on the world to-day? I do not wish to expand upon this theme. I had set out to make the apology of the professor speak for itself from a very circumstances of his work. But in these days, when money is everything, when pecuniary success is the only goal to be achieved, when the voice of the plutocrat is as the voice of God, the aspect of the professor, side-tracked in the real race of life, riding his mule of Padua in competition with an automobile, may at least help to soothe the others who have failed in the struggle.

Dare one, as the wildest of fancies, suggest how different things might be if learning counted, or if we could set it on its feet again, if students wanted to learn, and if professors had anything to teach, if a university lived for itself and not as a place of qualification for the junior employees of the rich; if there were only in this perplexing age some way of living humbly and retaining the respect of one's fellows; if a man with a few hundred dollars a year could cast out the money question and the house question, and the whole business of competitive appearances and live for the things of the mind! But then, after all, if the mind as a speculative instrument has gone bankrupt, if learning, instead of meaning a mind full of thought, means only a bellyful of fact, one is brought to a full stop, standing among the littered debris of an ideal that has passed away.

In any case the question, if it is one, is going to settle itself. The professor is passing away. The cost of living has laid its hold upon him, and grips him in its coils; within another generation he will be starved out, frozen out, 'evoluted' out by that glorious process of natural selection and adaptation, the rigour of which is the only God left in our desolated Pantheon. The male school-teacher is gone, the male clerk is going, and already on the horizon of the academic market rises the Woman with the Spectacles, the rude survivalist who, in the coming generation, will dispense the elements of learning cut to order, without an afterthought of what it once has meant.

The devil and the deep sea:

A discussion of modern morality

THE DEVIL is passing out of fashion. After a long and honourable career he has fallen into an ungrateful oblivion. His existence has become shadowy, his outline attenuated, and his personality displeasing to a complacent generation. So he stands now leaning on the handle of his three-pronged oyster fork and looking into the ashes of his smothered fire. Theology will have none of him. Genial clergy of ample girth, stuffed with the buttered toast of rectory tea, are preaching him out of existence. The fires of his material hell are replaced by the steam heat of moral torture. This even the most sensitive of sinners faces with equanimity. So the Devil's old dwelling is dismantled and stands by the roadside with a sign-board bearing the legend, 'Museum of Moral Torment, These Premises to Let.' In front of it, in place of the dancing imp of earlier ages, is a poor make-believe thing, a jack-o'lantern on a stick, with a turnip head and candle eyes, labelled 'Demon of Moral Repentance, Guaranteed Worse than Actual Fire.' The poor thing grins in its very harmlessness.

Now that the Devil is passing away an unappreciative generation fails to realise the high social function that he once performed. There he stood for ages a simple and workable basis of human morality; an admirable first-hand reason for being good, which needed no ulterior explanation. The rude peasant of the Middle Ages, the illiterate artisan of the shop, and the long-haired hind of the fields, had no need to speculate upon the problem of existence and the tangled skein of moral enquiry. The Devil took all that off their hands. He had either to 'be good' or else he 'got the fork,' just as in our time the unsuccessful comedian of amateur night in the vaudeville houses 'gets the hook.' Humanity, with the Devil to prod it from behind, moved steadily upwards on the path of moral development. Then having attained a certain elevation, it turned upon its tracks, denied that there had been any Devil, rubbed itself for a moment by way of investigation, said that there had been no prodding, and then fell to wandering about on the hill-tops without any fixed idea of goal or direction.

In other words, with the disappearance of the Devil there still remains unsolved the problem of conduct, and behind it the riddle of the universe. How are we getting along without the Devil? How are we managing to be good without the fork? What is happening to our conception of goodness itself?

To begin with, let me disclaim any intention of writing of
morality from the point of view of the technical, or professional,
moral philosopher. Such a person would settle the whole question
by a few references to pragmatism, transcendentalism, and esoteric
synthesis — leaving his auditors angry but unable to retaliate. This
attitude, I am happy to say, I am quite unable to adopt. I do not
know what pragmatism is, and I do not care. I know the word
transcendental only in connexion with advertisements for 'gents'
furnishings.' If Kant, or Schopenhauer, or Anheuser Busch have
already settled these questions, I cannot help it.

In any case, it is my opinion that now-a-days we are overridden in
the specialties, each in his own department of learning, with his tags,
and label, and his pigeon-hole category of proper names, precluding
all discussion by ordinary people. No man may speak fittingly of the
soul without spending at least six weeks in a theological college;
morality is the province of the moral philosopher who is prepared to
pelt the intruder back over the fence with a shower of German
commentaries. Ignorance, in its wooden shoes, shuffles around the
portico of the temple of learning, stumbling among the litter of
terminology. The broad field of human wisdom has been cut into a
multitude of little professorial rabbit warrens. In each of these a
specialist burrows deep, scratching out a shower of terminology,
head down in an unlovely attitude which places an interlocutor at a
grotesque conversational disadvantage.

May I digress a minute to show what I mean by the inconvenience
of modern learning? This happened at a summer boarding-house
where I spent a portion of the season of rest, in company with a
certain number of ordinary, ignorant people like myself. We got on
well together. In the evenings on the verandah we talked of nature
and of its beauties, of the stars and why they were so far away — we
didn't know their names, thank goodness — and such-like simple
topics of conversation.

Sometimes under the influence of a double-shotted sentimental-
ism sprung from huckleberry pie and doughnuts, we even spoke of
the larger issues of life, and exchanged opinions on immortality. We
used no technical terms. We knew none. The talk was harmless and
happy. Then there came among us a faded man in a coat that had
been black before it turned green, who was a PH D of Oberlin
College. The first night he sat on the verandah, somebody said how

beautiful the sunset was. Then the man from Oberlin spoke up and said: 'Yes, one could almost fancy it a pre-Raphaelite conception with the same chiaroscuro in the atmosphere.' There was a pause. That ended all nature study for almost an hour. Later in the evening, some one who had been reading a novel said in simple language that he was sick of having the hero always come out on top. 'Ah,' said the man from Oberlin, 'but doesn't that precisely correspond with Nitch's idea (he meant, I suppose, Nietzsche, but he pronounced it to rhyme with "bitch") of the dominance of man over fate?' Mr Hezekiah Smith who kept the resort looked round admiringly and said, 'Ain't he a *terr?*' He certainly was. While the man from Oberlin stayed with us, elevating conversation was at an end, and a self-conscious ignorance hung upon the verandah like a fog.

However, let us get back to the Devil. Let us notice in the first place that because we have kicked out the Devil as an absurd and ridiculous superstition, unworthy of a scientific age, we have by no means eliminated the super-natural and the super-rational from the current thought of our time. I suppose there never was an age more riddled with superstition, more credulous, more drunkenly addicted to thaumaturgy than the present. The Devil in his palmiest days was nothing to it. In despite of our vaunted material common-sense, there is a perfect craving abroad for belief in something beyond the compass of the believable.

It shows itself in every age and class. Simpering Seventeen gets its fortune told on a weighing machine, and shudders with luxurious horror at the prospective villainy of the Dark Man who is to cross her life. Senile Seventy gravely sits on a wooden bench at a wonder-working meeting, waiting for a gentleman in a 'Tuxedo' jacket to call up the soul of Napoleon Bonaparte, and ask its opinion of Mr Taft. Here you have a small tenement, let us say, on South Clark St, Chicago. What is it? It is the home of Nadir the Nameless, the great Hindoo astrologer. Who are in the front room? Clients waiting for a revelation of the future. Where is Nadir? He is behind a heavily draped curtain, worked with Indian serpents. By the waiting clients Nadir is understood to be in consultation with the twin fates, Isis and Osiris. In reality Nadir is frying potatoes. Presently he will come out from behind the curtain and announce that Osiris has spoken (that is, the potatoes are now finished and on the back of the stove) and that he is prepared to reveal hidden treasure at 40 cents a revelation. Marvellous, is it not, this Hindoo astrology business? And any one can be a Nadir the Nameless, who cares to stain his face blue with thimbleberry juice, wrap a red turban round his forehead, and cut the rate of revelation to 35 cents. Such is the credulity of the age which has repudiated the Devil as too difficult of belief.

We have, it is true, moved far away from the Devil; but are we after all so much better off? or do we, in respect of the future, contain within ourselves the promise of better things. I suppose that most of us would have the general idea that there never was an age which displayed so high a standard of morality, or at least of ordinary human decency, as our own. We look back with a shudder to the blood-stained history of our ancestors; the fires of Smithfield with the poor martyr writhing about his post, frenzied and hysterical in the flames; the underground cell where the poor remnant of humanity turned its haggard face to the torch of the entering goaler; the madhouse itself with its gibbering occupants converted into a show for the idle fools of London. We may well look back on it all and say that, at least, we are better than we were. The history of our little human race would make but sorry reading were not its every page imprinted with the fact that human ingenuity has invented no torment too great for human fortitude to bear.

In general decency — sympathy — we have undoubtedly progressed. Our courts of law have forgotten the use of the thumbkins and boot; we do not press a criminal under 'weights greater than he can bear' in order to induce him to plead; nor flog to ribbands the bleeding back of the malefactor dragged at the cart's tail through the thoroughfares of a crowded city. Our public, objectionable though it is, as it fights its way to its ball games, breathes peanuts and peppermint upon the offended atmosphere, and shrieks aloud its chronic and collective hysteria, is at all events better than the leering oafs of the Elizabethan century, who put hard-boiled eggs in their pockets and sat around upon the grass waiting for the 'burning' to begin.

But when we have admitted that we are better than we were as far as the *facts* of our moral conduct go, we may well ask as to the principles upon which our conduct is based. In past ages there was the authoritative moral code as a guide — thou shalt and thou shalt not — and behind it the pains, and the penalties, and the three-pronged oyster-fork. Under that influence, humanity, or a large part

of it, slowly and painfully acquired the moral habit. At present it
goes on, as far as its actions are concerned, with the momentum of
the old beliefs.

But when we turn from the actions on the surface to the ideas
underneath, we find in our time a strange confusion of beliefs out of
which is presently to be made the New Morality. Let us look at some
of the varied ideas manifested in the cross sections of the moral
tendencies of our time.

Here we have first of all the creed and cult of self-development. It
arrogates to itself the title of New Thought, but contains in reality
nothing but the Old Selfishness. According to this particular outlook
the goal of morality is found in fully developing one's self. Be large,
says the votary of this creed, be high, be broad. He gives a shilling to
a starving man, not that the man may be fed but that he himself may
be a shilling-giver. He cultivates sympathy with the destitute for the
sake of being sympathetic. The whole of his virtue and his creed of
conduct runs to a cheap and easy egomania in which his blind
passion for himself causes him to use external people and things as
mere reactions upon his own personality. The immoral little toad
swells itself to the bursting point in its desire to be a moral ox.

In its more ecstatic form, this creed expresses itself in a sort of
general feeling of 'uplift,' or the desire for internal moral expansion.
The votary is haunted by the idea of his own elevation. He wants to
get into touch with nature, to swim in the Greater Being, 'to tune
himself,' harmonise himself, and generally to perform on himself as
on a sort of moral accordion. He gets himself somehow mixed up
with natural objects, with the sadness of autumn, falls with the
leaves and drips with the dew. Were it not for the complacent
self-sufficiency which he induces, his refined morality might easily
verge into simple idiocy. Yet, odd though it may seem, this creed of
self-development struts about with its head high as one of the chief
moral factors which have replaced the authoritative dogma of the
older time.

The vague and hysterical desire to 'uplift' one's self merely for
exaltation's sake is about as effective an engine of moral progress as
the effort to lift one's self in the air by a terrific hitching up of the
breeches.

The same creed has its physical side. It parades the Body, with a
capital B, as also a thing that must be developed; and this, not for

any ulterior thing that may be effected by it but presumably as an end in itself. The Monk or the Good Man of the older day despised the body as a thing that must learn to know its betters. He spiked it down with a hair shirt to teach it the virtue of submission. He was of course very wrong and very objectionable. But one doubts if he was much worse than his modern successor who joys consciously in the operation of his pores and his glands, and the correct rhythmical contraction of his abdominal muscles, as if he constituted simply a sort of superior sewerage system.

I once knew a man called Juggins who exemplified this point of view. He used to ride a bicycle every day to train his muscles and to clear his brain. He looked at all the scenery that he passed to develop his taste for scenery. He gave to the poor to develop his sympathy with poverty. He read the Bible regularly in order to cultivate the faculty of reading the Bible, and visited picture galleries with painful assiduity in order to give himself a feeling for art. He passed through life with a strained and haunted expression waiting for clarity of intellect, greatness of soul, and a passion for art to descend upon him like a flock of doves. He is now dead. He died presumably in order to cultivate the sense of being a corpse.

No doubt, in the general scheme or purpose of things the cult of self-development and the botheration about the Body may, through the actions which it induces, be working for a good end. It plays a part, no doubt, in whatever is to be the general evolution of morality.

And there, in that very word evolution, we are brought face to face with another of the wide-spread creeds of our day, which seek to replace the older. This one is not so much a guide to conduct as a theory, and a particularly cheap and easy one, of a general meaning and movement of morality. The person of this persuasion is willing to explain everything in terms of its having been once something else and being about to pass into something further still. Evolution, as the natural scientists know it, is a plain and straightforward matter, not so much a theory as a view of a succession of facts taken in organic relation. It assumes no purposes whatever. It is not — if I may be allowed a professor's luxury of using a word which will not be understood — in any degree teleological.

The social philosopher who adopts the evolutionary theory of morals is generally one who is quite in the dark as to the true conception of evolution itself. He understands from Darwin, Huxley, and other great writers whom he has not read, that the animals have been fashioned into their present shape by a long process of twisting, contortion, and selection, at once laborious and deserving. The giraffe lengthened its neck by conscientious stretching; the frog webbed its feet by perpetual swimming; and the bird broke out in feathers by unremitting flying. 'Nature' by weeding out the short giraffe, the inadequate frog, and the top-heavy bird encouraged by selection the ones most 'fit to survive.' Hence the origin of species, the differentiation of organs – hence, in fact, everything.

Here, too, when the theory is taken over and mis-translated from pure science to the humanities, is found the explanation of all our social and moral growth. Each of our religious customs is like the giraffe's neck. A manifestation such as the growth of Christianity is regarded as if humanity broke out into a new social organism, in the same way as the ascending amoeba breaks out into a stomach. With this view of human relations, nothing in the past is said to be either good or bad. Everything is a movement. Cannibalism is a sort of apprenticeship in meat-eating. The institution of slavery is seen as an evolutionary stage towards free citizenship, and 'Uncle Tom's' over-seer is no longer a nigger-driver but a social force tending towards the survival of the Booker Washington type of negro.

With his brain saturated with the chloroform of this social dogma, the moral philosopher ceases to be able to condemn anything at all, measures all things with a centimetre scale of his little doctrine, and finds them all of the same length. Whereupon he presently desists from thought altogether, calls everything bad or good an evolution, and falls asleep with his hands folded upon his stomach murmuring, 'survival of the fittest.'

Anybody who will look at the thing candidly, will see that the evolutionary explanation of morals is meaningless, and presupposes the existence of the very thing it ought to prove. It starts from a misconception of the biological doctrine. Biology has nothing to say as to what ought to survive and what ought not to survive; it merely speaks of what does survive. The burdock easily kills the violet, and the Canadian skunk lingers where the humming-bird has died. In biology the test of fitness to survive is the fact of the survival itself – nothing else. To apply this doctrine to the moral field brings out grotesque results. The successful burglar ought to be presented by society with a nickel-plated 'jimmy,' and the starving cripple left to die in the ditch. Everything – any phase of movement or religion – which succeeds, is right. Anything which does not is wrong. Everything which is, is right; everything which was, is right; everything which will be, is right. All we have to do is to sit still and watch it come. This is moral evolution.

On such a basis, we might expect to find, as the general outcome of the new moral code now in the making, the simple worship of success. This is exactly what is happening. The morality which the Devil with his oyster fork was commissioned to inculcate was essentially altruistic. Things were to be done for other people. The new ideas, if you combine them in a sort of moral amalgam – to develop one's self, to evolve, to measure things by their success – weigh on the other side of the scale. So it comes about that the scale begins to turn and the new morality shows signs of exalting the old-fashioned Badness in place of the discredited Goodness. Hence we find, saturating our contemporary literature, the new worship of the Strong Man, the easy pardon of the Unscrupulous, the Apotheosis of the Jungle, and the Deification of the Detective. Force, brute force, is what we now turn to as the moral ideal, and Mastery and Success are the sole tests of excellence. The nation cuddles its multi-millionaires, cinematographs itself silly with the pictures of its prize fighters, and even casts an eye of slantwise admiration through the bars of its penitentiaries. Beside these things the simple Good Man of the older dispensation, with his worn alpaca coat and his obvious inefficiency, is nowhere.

Truly, if we go far enough with it, the Devil may come to his own again, and more than his own, not merely as Head Stoker but as what is called an End in Himself.

I knew a little man called Bliggs. He worked in a railroad office, a simple, dusty, little man, harmless at home and out of it till he read of Napoleon and heard of the thing called a Superman. Then somebody told him of Nitch, and he read as much Nitch as he could understand. The thing went to his head. Morals were no longer for him. He used to go home from the office and be a Superman by the hour, curse if his dinner was late, and strut the length of his little home with a silly irritation which he mistook for moral enfranchisement. Presently he took to being a Superman in business hours, and the railroad dismissed him. They know nothing of Nitch in such crude places. It has often seemed to me that Bliggs typified much of the present moral movement.

Our poor Devil then is gone. We cannot have him back for the whistling. For generations, as yet unlearned in social philosophy, he played a useful part — a dual part in a way, for it was his function to illustrate at once the pleasures and the penalties of life. Merriment in the scheme of things was his, and for those drawn too far in pleasure and merriment, retribution and the oyster fork.

I can see him before me now, his long, eager face and deep-set, brown eyes, pathetic with the failure of ages — carrying with him his pack of cards, his amber flask, and his little fiddle. Let but the door of the cottage stand open upon a winter night, and the Devil would blow in, offering his flask and fiddle, or rattling his box of dice.

So with his twin incentives of pain and pleasure he coaxed and prodded humanity on its path, till it reached the point where it repudiated him, called itself a Superman, and headed straight for the cliff over which is the deep sea. *Quo vadimus?*

The Woman Question

I WAS sitting the other day in what is called the Peacock Alley
of one of our leading hotels, drinking tea with another thing like
myself, a man. At the next table were a group of Superior Beings in
silk, talking. I couldn't help overhearing what they said — at least
not when I held my head a little sideways.

They were speaking of the war.

'There wouldn't have been any war,' said one, 'if women were
allowed to vote.'

'No, indeed,' chorused all the others.

The woman who had spoken looked about her defiantly. She
wore spectacles and was of the type that we men used to call, in
days when we still retained a little courage, an Awful Woman.

'When women have the vote,' she went on, 'there will be no more
war. The women will forbid it.'

She gazed about her angrily. She evidently wanted to be heard.
My friend and I hid ourselves behind a little fern and trembled.

But we listened. We were hoping that the Awful Woman would
explain how war would be ended. She didn't. She went on to explain
instead that when women have the vote there will be no more
poverty, no disease, no germs, no cigarette smoking and nothing to
drink but water.

It seemed a gloomy world.

'Come,' whispered my friend, 'this is no place for us. Let us go to
the bar.'

'No,' I said, 'leave me. I am going to write an article on the
Woman Question. The time has come when it has got to be taken up
and solved.'

So I set myself to write it.

The woman problem may be stated somewhat after this fashion.
The great majority of the women of to-day find themselves without
any means of support of their own. I refer of course to the civilised
white women. The gay savage in her jungle, attired in a cocoanut
leaf, armed with a club and adorned with the neck of a soda-water
bottle, is all right. Trouble hasn't reached her yet. Like all savages,
she has a far better time — more varied, more interesting, more
worthy of a human being — than falls to the lot of the rank and file
of civilised men and women. Very few of us recognise this great
truth. We have a mean little vanity over our civilisation. We are
touchy about it. We do not realise that so far we have done little but

increase the burden of work and multiply the means of death. But for the hope of better things to come, our civilisation would not seem worth while.

But this is a digression. Let us go back. The great majority of women have no means of support of their own. This is true also of men. But the men can acquire means of support. They can hire themselves out and work. Better still, by the industrious process of intrigue rightly called 'busyness,' or business, they may presently get hold of enough of other people's things to live without working. Or again, men can, with a fair prospect of success, enter the criminal class, either in its lower ranks as a house breaker, or in its upper ranks, through politics. Take it all in all a man has a certain chance to get along in life.

A woman, on the other hand, has little or none. The world's work is open to her, but she cannot do it. She lacks the physical strength for laying bricks or digging coal. If put to work on a steel beam a hundred feet above the ground, she would fall off. For the pursuit of business her head is all wrong. Figures confuse her. She lacks sustained attention and in point of morals the average woman is, even for business, too crooked.

This last point is one that will merit a little emphasis. Men are queer creatures. They are able to set up a code of rules or a standard, often quite an artificial one, and stick to it. They have acquired the art of playing the game. Eleven men can put on white flannel trousers and call themselves a cricket team, on which an entirely new set of obligations, almost a new set of personalities, are wrapped about them. Women could never be a team of anything.

So it is in business. Men are able to maintain a sort of rough and ready code which prescribes the particular amount of cheating that a man may do under the rules. This is called business honesty, and many men adhere to it with a dog-like tenacity, growing old in it, till it is stamped on their grizzled faces, visibly. They can feel it inside them like a virtue. So much will they cheat and no more. Hence men are able to trust one another, knowing the exact degree of dishonesty they are entitled to expect.

With women it is entirely different. They bring to business an unimpaired vision. They see it as it is. It would be impossible to trust them. They refuse to play fair.

Thus it comes about that woman is excluded, to a great extent, from the world's work and the world's pay.

There is nothing really open to her except one thing – marriage. She must find a man who will be willing, in return for her society, to give her half of everything he has, allow her the sole use of his house during the daytime, pay her taxes, and provide her clothes.

This was, formerly and for many centuries, not such a bad solution of the question. The women did fairly well out of it. It was the habit to marry early and often. The 'house and home' was an important place. The great majority of people, high and low, lived on the land. The work of the wife and the work of the husband ran closely together. The two were complementary and fitted into one another. A woman who had to superintend the baking of bread and the brewing of beer, the spinning of yarn and the weaving of clothes, could not complain that her life was incomplete.

Then came the modern age, beginning let us say about a hundred and fifty years ago. The distinguishing marks of it have been machinery and the modern city. The age of invention swept the people off the land. It herded them into factories, creating out of each man a poor miserable atom divorced from hereditary ties, with no rights, no duties, and no place in the world except what his wages contract may confer on him. Every man for himself, and sink or swim, became the order of the day. It was nicknamed 'industrial freedom.' The world's production increased enormously. It is doubtful if the poor profited much. They obtained the modern city – full of light and noise and excitement, lively with crime and gay with politics – and the free school where they learned to read and write, by which means they might hold a mirror to their poverty and take a good look at it. They lost the quiet of the country side, the murmur of the brook and the inspiration of the open sky. These are unconscious things, but the peasant who has been reared among them, for all his unconsciousness, pines and dies without them. It is doubtful if the poor have gained. The chaw-bacon rustic who trimmed a hedge in the reign of George the First, compares well with the pale slum-rat of the reign of George v.

But if the machine age has profoundly altered the position of the working man, it has done still more with woman. It has dispossessed her. Her work has been taken away. The machine does it. It makes the clothes and brews the beer. The roar of the vacuum cleaner has hushed the sound of the broom. The proud proportions of the old-time cook, are dwindled to the slim outline of the gas-stove expert operating on a beefsteak with the aid of a thermometer. And at the close of day the machine, wound with a little key, sings the modern infant to its sleep, with the faultless lullaby of the Victrola. The home has passed, or at least is passing out of existence. In place of it is the 'apartment' – an incomplete thing, a mere part of something, where children are an intrusion, where hospitality is done through a caterer, and where Christmas is only the twenty-fifth of December.

All this the machine age did for woman. For a time she suffered – the one thing she had learned, in the course of centuries, to do with admirable fitness. With each succeeding decade of the modern age things grew worse instead of better. The age for marriage shifted. A wife instead of being a help-mate had become a burden that must be carried. It was no longer true that two could live on less than one. The prudent youth waited till he could 'afford' a wife. Love itself grew timid. Little Cupid exchanged his bow and arrow for a book on arithmetic and studied money sums. The school girl who flew to Gretna Green in a green and yellow cabriolet beside a peach-faced youth – angrily pursued by an ancient father of thirty-eight – all this drifted into the pictures of the past, romantic but quite impossible.

Thus the unmarried woman, a quite distinct thing from the 'old maid' of ancient times, came into existence, and multiplied and increased till there were millions of her.

Then there rose up in our own time, or within call of it, a deliverer. It was the Awful Woman with the Spectacles, and the doctrine that she preached was Woman's Rights. She came as a new thing, a hatchet in her hand, breaking glass. But in reality she was no new thing at all, and had her lineal descent in history from age to age. The Romans knew her as a sybil and shuddered at her. The Middle Ages called her a witch and burnt her. The ancient law of England named her a scold and ducked her in a pond. But the men of the modern age, living indoors and losing something of their ruder fibre, grew afraid of her. The Awful Woman – meddlesome, vociferous, intrusive – came into her own.

Her softer sisters followed her. She became the leader of her sex. 'Things are all wrong,' she screamed, 'with the *status* of women.' Therein she was quite right. 'The remedy for it all,' she howled, 'is to make women "free," to give women the vote. When once women are

"free" everything will be all right.' Therein the woman with the
spectacles was, and is, utterly wrong.

The women's vote, when they get it, will leave women much as
they were before.

Let it be admitted quite frankly that women are going to get the
vote. Within a very short time all over the British Isles and North
America – in the States and the nine provinces of Canada – woman
suffrage will soon be an accomplished fact. It is a coming event
which casts its shadow, or its illumination, in front of it. The
woman's vote and total prohibition are two things that are moving
across the map with gigantic strides. Whether they are good or bad
things is another question. They are coming. As for the women's
vote, it has largely come. And as for prohibition, it is going to be
recorded as one of the results of the European War, foreseen by
nobody. When the King of England decided that the way in which
he could best help the country was by giving up drinking, the
admission was fatal. It will stand as one of the landmarks of British
history comparable only to such things as the signing of the Magna
Carta by King John, or the serving out of rum and water instead of
pure rum in the British Navy under George III.

So the woman's vote and prohibition are coming. A few rare
spots – such as Louisiana, and the City of New York – will remain
and offer here and there a wet oasis in the desert of dry virtue. Even
that cannot endure. Before many years are past, all over this continent women with a vote and men without a drink will stand
looking at one another and wondering, what next?

For when the vote is reached the woman question will not be
solved but only begun. In and of itself, a vote is nothing. It neither
warms the skin nor fills the stomach. Very often the privilege of a
vote confers nothing but the right to express one's opinion as to
which of two crooks is the crookeder.

But after the women have obtained the vote the question is, what
are they going to do with it? The answer is, nothing, or at any rate
nothing that men would not do without them. Their only visible use
of it will be to elect men into office. Fortunately for us all they will
not elect women. Here and there perhaps at the outset, it will be
done as the result of a sort of spite, a kind of sex antagonism bred
by the controversy itself. But, speaking broadly, the women's vote
will not be used to elect women to office. Women do not think

enough of one another to do that. If they want a lawyer they consult a man, and those who can afford it have their clothes made by men, and their cooking done by a chef. As for their money, no woman would entrust that to another woman's keeping. They are far too wise for that.

So the woman's vote will not result in the setting up of female prime ministers and of parliaments in which the occupants of the treasury bench cast languishing eyes across at the flushed faces of the opposition. From the utter ruin involved in such an attempt at mixed government, the women themselves will save us. They will elect men. They may even pick some good ones. It is a nice question and will stand thinking about.

But what else, or what further can they do, by means of their vote and their representatives to 'emancipate' and 'liberate' their sex?

Many feminists would tell us at once that if women had the vote they would, first and foremost, throw everything open to women on the same terms as men. Whole speeches are made on this point, and a fine fury thrown into it, often very beautiful to behold.

The entire idea is a delusion. Practically all of the world's work is open to women now, wide open. *The only trouble is that they can't do it.* There is nothing to prevent a woman from managing a bank, or organising a company, or running a department store, or floating a merger, or building a railway — except the simple fact that she can't. Here and there an odd woman does such things, but she is only the exception that proves the rule. Such women are merely — and here I am speaking in the most decorous biological sense — 'sports.' The ordinary woman cannot do the ordinary man's work. She never has and never will. The reasons why she can't are so many, that is, she *'can't'* in so many different ways, that it is not worth while to try to name them.

Here and there it is true there are things closed to women, not by their own inability but by the law. This is a gross injustice. There is no defence for it. The province in which I live, for example, refuses to allow women to practise as lawyers. This is wrong. Women have just as good a right to fail at being lawyers as they have at anything else. But even if all these legal disabilities, where they exist, were removed (as they will be under a woman's vote) the difference to women at large will be infinitesimal. A few gifted 'sports' will earn a handsome livelihood, but the woman question in the larger sense will not move one inch nearer to solution.

The feminists, in fact, are haunted by the idea that it is possible for the average woman to have a life patterned after that of the ordinary man. They imagine her as having a career, a profession, a vocation — something which will be her 'life work' — just as selling coal is the life work of the coal merchant.

If this were so, the whole question would be solved. Women and men would become equal and independent. It is thus indeed that the feminist sees them, through the roseate mist created by imagination. Husband and wife appear as a couple of honourable partners who share a house together. Each is off to business in the morning. The husband is, let us say, a stock broker: the wife manufactures iron and steel. The wife is a Liberal, the husband a Conservative. At their dinner they have animated discussions over the tariff till it is time for them to go to their clubs.

These two impossible creatures haunt the brain of the feminist and disport them in the pages of the up-to-date novel.

The whole thing is mere fiction. It is quite impossible for women — the average and ordinary women — to go in for having a career. Nature has forbidden it. The average woman must necessarily have — I can only give the figures roughly — about three and a quarter children. She must replace in the population herself and her husband with something over to allow for the people who never marry and for the children that do not reach maturity. If she fails to do this the population comes to an end. Any scheme of social life must allow for these three and a quarter children and for the years of care that must be devoted to them. The vacuum cleaner can take the place of the housewife. It cannot replace the mother. No man ever said his prayers at the knees of a vacuum cleaner, or drew his first lessons in manliness and worth from the sweet old-fashioned stories that a vacuum cleaner told. Feminists of the enraged kind may talk as they will of the paid attendant and the expert baby-minder. Fiddlesticks! These things are a mere supplement, useful enough but as far away from the realities of motherhood as the vacuum cleaner itself. But the point is one that need not be labour-ed. Sensible people understand it as soon as said. With fools it is not worth while to argue.

But, it may be urged, there are, even as it is, a great many women who are working. The wages that they receive are extremely low. They are lower in most cases than the wages for the same, or similar work, done by men. Cannot the woman's vote at least remedy this?

Here is something that deserves thinking about and that is far more nearly within the realm of what is actual and possible than wild talk of equalising and revolutionising the sexes.

It is quite true that women's work is underpaid. But this is only a part of a larger social injustice.

The case stands somewhat as follows: Women get low wages because low wages are all that they are worth. Taken by itself this is a brutal and misleading statement. What is meant is this. The rewards and punishments in the unequal and ill-adjusted world in which we live are most unfair. The price of anything — sugar, potatoes, labour, or anything else — varies according to the supply and demand: if many people want it and few can supply it the price goes up: if the contrary it goes down. If enough cabbages are brought to market they will not bring a cent a piece, no matter what it cost to raise them.

On these terms each of us sells his labour. The lucky ones, with some rare gift, or trained capacity, or some ability that by mere circumstance happens to be in a great demand, can sell high. If there were only one night plumber in a great city, and the water pipes in a dozen homes of a dozen millionaires should burst all at once, he might charge a fee like that of a consulting lawyer.

On the other hand the unlucky sellers whose numbers are greater than the demand — the mass of common labourers — get a mere pittance. To say that their wage represents all that they produce is to argue in a circle. It is the mere pious quietism with which the well-to-do man who is afraid to think boldly on social questions drugs his conscience to sleep.

So it stands with women's wages. It is the sheer numbers of the women themselves, crowding after the few jobs that they can do, that brings them down. It has nothing to do with the attitude of men collectively towards women in the lump. It cannot be remedied by any form of woman's freedom. Its remedy is bound up with the general removal of social injustice, the general abolition of poverty, which is to prove the great question of the century before us. The question of women's wages is a part of the wages' question.

To my thinking the whole idea of making women free and equal (politically) with men as a way of improving their *status,* starts from a wrong basis and proceeds in a wrong direction.

Women need not more freedom but less. Social policy should proceed from the fundamental truth that women are and must be dependent. If they cannot be looked after by an individual (a thing on which they took their chance in earlier days) they must be looked after by the State. To expect a woman, for example, if left by the death of her husband with young children without support, to maintain herself by her own efforts, is the most absurd mockery of freedom ever devised. Earlier generations of mankind, for all that they lived in the jungle and wore cocoanut leaves, knew nothing of it. To turn a girl loose in the world to work for herself, when there is no work to be had, or none at a price that will support life, is a social crime.

I am not attempting to show in what way the principle of woman's dependence should be worked out in detail in legislation. Nothing short of a book could deal with it. All that the present essay attempts is the presentation of a point of view.

I have noticed that my clerical friends, on the rare occasions when they are privileged to preach to me, have a way of closing their sermons by 'leaving their congregations with a thought.' It is a good scheme. It suggests an inexhaustible fund of reserve thought not yet tapped. It keeps the congregation, let us hope, in a state of trembling eagerness for the next instalment.

With the readers of this essay I do the same. I leave them with the thought that perhaps in the modern age it is not the increased freedom of woman that is needed but the increased recognition of their dependence. Let the reader remain agonised over that till I write something else.

The tyranny of prohibition

THE WHOLE of North America, or all of it that lies between the
Mexicans and the Esquimaux, is passing under a new tyranny. It is
new, at least, in the sense that the particular form of it, under the
name of Prohibition, is a thing hitherto unknown in the world. It is
old in the sense that the evil that inspires it is that against which for
ages the spirit of liberty has been in conflict.

It is time that people in England should have proper warning of
the social catastrophe which has overwhelmed America. While there
is yet time the danger should be averted. For the United States and
Canada regret is too late. It is only too evident now that the proper
time for protest and opposition was at the beginning of the insidious
movement. But few people realized the power of fanaticism or the
peculiar weaknesses of democratic rule upon which it fed. From the
crusade of a despised minority, a mark for good-natured ridicule
rather than fear, the prohibition movement became a vast continental propaganda, backed by unlimited money, engineered by
organized hypocrisy. Under the stress of war it masqueraded as the
crowning effort of patriotism. The war over, it sits enthroned as a
social tyranny, backed by the full force of the law, the like of which
has not been seen in English-speaking countries since the fires died
out at Smithfield.

The precise legislative situation at the present moment is this. In
the United States sixteen of the forty-eight states are 'bone-dry'; this
means that in these states 'liquor' can neither be sold nor can it be
brought in by the individual citizen from outside. Eighteen other
states are 'dry'; in these no liquor can be sold, but it may be
imported. In these states, Brother Stiggins, while deploring with
uplifted hands and eyes the evils of the liquor traffic, can still order
in a comfortable little keg from the outside. The other fourteen
states are still 'wet.' In this category belong Massachusetts, New
York, Pennsylvania, Connecticut, and Louisiana, states typical of the
old culture of the country; while, by a strange freak of psychology,
the wilder and woolier of the states are found among the list of the
dry. Oklahoma, the latest flower of the prairies, is dry as a bone. In
Idaho, even the possession of 'liquor' in a private cellar is a crime.
Nevada is as dry as its own desert. Moreover, even the 'wet' states are
spotted over with the arid areas of 'local option' municipalities that
have dried up of their own local volition. In Kentucky one hundred
and seven counties out of one hundred and twenty are dry.

California, spurning the pleasant vineyards of its hillsides, is half dry. Missouri announces itself as 'fifty-three per cent dry,' showing a majority, at least, on the side of virtue.

But all of this only represents the least part of the situation. When the nation sprang to arms in April 1917, the prohibitionist sprang upon the platform. A War-Time Prohibition Act was passed through Congress making the whole country dry from July 1, 1919, till the demobilizing of the armies after the coming of peace. Finally, to crown the work, an amendment to the Federal constitution was proposed by the Congress by the necessary two-thirds vote, and was passed into the State Legislatures for ratification. Under the law amendments need the sanction of two-thirds of the State Legislatures. The necessary thirty-six states had ratified by January 20, 1919, and the amendment is to come into force on January 20, 1920. Its terms are complete and all-enveloping as the darkness of an eclipse

After one year from the ratification of this article the manufacture, sale, or transportation of intoxicating liquors within, the importation thereof into, or the exportation thereof from, the United States and all territory subject to the jurisdiction thereof, for beverage purposes, is hereby prohibited.

From this amendment there is no way out. A counter-amendment to abolish it would involve the action of both Houses of Congress, of thirty-six State Legislatures, each made up of two Houses. Such a concurrence is outside of the bounds of practical politics. The door is locked and the key is thrown away.

So much for the United States. A similar situation obtains in Canada. Here all of the nine Provinces have voted themselves dry. The dryness is actually in force in eight of them. The Province of Quebec, unable, in spite of its French population, to stand alone against the contagion of a continent, dried up on May 1 of 1919. Superimposed on the Provincial legislation is that of the Federal Government of the Dominion of Canada. Under the War Measures Act a Federal Order in Council prohibits all import and transportation of intoxicating liquor.

Here and there, indeed, the Canadian situation presents some redeeming features. Thus, Quebec is to hold a referendum as to whether the prohibition shall be total or shall permit the sale of thin beer and even thinner wine. But the beer – defined with scientific cruelty under the law – is to be lighter than German lager, and the wine is to be less maddening than claret. In Ontario, also, the present law provides for a referendum before a final acceptance of the system. There is talk, too, of a general Federal referendum to be taken by the Dominion Government. But there is little hope that the return to common sense and the revulsion against fanaticism will be rapid enough to prevent the catastrophe.

A candid outsider might well stand perplexed as to how and why communities apparently free can vote themselves into such an appalling bondage. The reasons for it can only be understood by an appreciation of certain of the peculiar features, certain characteristic weaknesses of democracy in North America. Both in the United States and in Canada we have long since fallen under the administration of the class of people whom we call the 'politicians.' Let it be noted that the word *administration* just used is employed designedly: we are not and never have been under the *rule* of the politicians. They have never wanted to rule. They do not lead, they follow. They do not speak, they listen. They do not move, they are pushed. What the politician wants is the emolument and the dignity of office and the elusive appearance of power: a certain number, too, are seeking the opportunity of more sinister gains. But the real governing forces in North America are such things as Big Business, the Manufacturers, the Labor Unions, and, in various forms National Hysteria mixed in with it all, as the war has proved, is the golden thread of individual patriotism and love of country, woven into the complex meshes of national selfishness. On the whole, the rule is not bad: it is free at least from the arrogance of caste and the power of hereditary aristocracy that disfigures still the governments of the older world.

But the least part of it all, in the sense of real influence and power, is the politician: He moves about in his frock coat and his silk hat, a garb which he shares alone with the undertaker and the traveling conjurer, his pocket full of presentation cigars, the most meretricious and the most melancholy figure in the democracy of North America. At times, indeed, he bursts through the shell that envelops him and insists on being a leader in his own right, a ruler of men and not a suppliant for votes: as witness of such stands the commanding figure of a Roosevelt and the manly dignity of a Borden. But these are the exceptions. The ordinary politician is merely busy picking up his votes from the mud of democracy like the *ramasseur* of the Parisian streets picking up cigar butts.

Thus in the matter of real rule the politician is nowhere. His only aim is to give the public what the public wants or at least what the public seems to ask for. And the politician has heard apparently only a single voice. On the one hand were the prohibitionists — articulate, strident, fanatical, highly organized, amply supplied with money, with the name of religion upon their lips, ready at a moment's notice to lash themselves into a fit of hysteria, and to attack with over-whelming force the personal fortunes and the political position of anyone who should dare to oppose them. On the other side was the general public, the vast majority of whom were, and are, opposed to national prohibition, but among whom no individual, or at best only one or two in thousands, was prepared to take the risk of open opposition to the relentless and fanatical minority.

Where the public would not speak, the politician would not act. A great many ministers of the Crown in Canada, members of the Canadian Legislatures and of the State Assemblies of the United States, have recorded a silent vote in favor of prohibition with loathing and contempt for it in their hearts. I speak here of what I know. If proof were needed I could name such men: but in the atmosphere in which we live in Canada, to 'accuse' one's parliamentary friends of being opposed to prohibition would be about the same as to accuse them of being in favor of burglary.

Moreover, the method of operation of the prohibitionist has been singularly ingenious. There was no question at first of total national prohibition. The thing was done bit by bit. Municipalties voted themselves 'dry' with but little opposition. The individual citizen, still able to order his 'liquor' from the outside, gave but little heed to what was happening. Even when whole states and provinces dried up in response to the fanatical clamor of the minority, the citizens at large raised practically no protest. They could still 'get it from the outside.' They did not propose to worry. They did not realize that the time was coming when there would be no 'outside.'

Moreover, it has to be acknowledged that there are throughout the United States and Canada great numbers of people who are strongly in favor of prohibition for everybody except themselves.

The South went dry by the vote of the whites who proposed to keep drink away from the blacks, not for the sake of their souls, but in order to get more work out of them. The manufacturer voted his employees dry with the same expectation, proposing for himself to remain 'wet.' The shopkeepers of the towns voted the farmers dry, so as to get more money in trade. The farmers who live in the country where it is dark and silent, helped to vote the cities into dryness as a spite against their lights and gayety.

One might well ask who, then, are the real prohibitionists? Such there undoubtedly are. In the first place there are a certain number of deeply religious, patriotic, and estimable people who actually believe that in passing a law to make it a crime for a man to sell a glass of beer they are doing the work of Christ on earth. Let them be entitled — along with Torquemada and Philip of Spain — to the credit of their good intentions. Along with these are a vast number of people who are animated by the evil spirit that for ages long has vexed the fortunes of humanity: the desire to tyrannize and compel — to force the souls of other men to compliance with the narrow rigor of their own. These, above all, are the typical prohibitionists. But to their numbers must be added the large body of people who fish in the troubled waters for their own gain: the salaried enthusiasts, the paid informers, the politicians seeking for votes, ministers of the Gospel currying favor with the dominant section of their congregation, business men and proprietors of newspapers whose profit lies in the hands of the prohibitionists to make or mar. To all these must be added the whole cohort of drunkards who can be relied upon to poll a vote in favor of prohibition in a mood of sentimental remorse.

On the other side stand, undoubtedly, the great majority of the people. National prohibition, let it be observed, has not been adopted either in the United States or in Canada by a popular vote. It never would be. It has been carried only by the votes of the Legislatures, by the actions of the politicians responsive to the demand of the minority. But the great mass of the people took no action. There has grown up, indeed, among all those who ought to be the leaders of public opinion, a strange conspiracy of silence. Nobody seems willing to bear witness to how widely diffused is the habit of normal wholesome drinking, and of the great benefits to be derived from it. The university where I have worked for nearly twenty years contains in its faculties a great number of scholarly, industrious men whose life work cannot be derided or despised even by the salaried agitator of a prohibitionist society. Yet the great majority of them 'drink.' I use that awful word in the full gloomy sense given to it by the teetotaler. I mean that if you ask these men to dinner and offer them a glass of wine, they will take it. Some will take two. I have even seen them take Scotch and soda. During these same years I have been privileged to know a great many of the leading lawyers of Montreal, whose brains and energy and service to the community I cannot too much admire. If there are any of them who do not 'drink,' I can only say that I have not seen them. I can bear the same dreadful testimony on behalf of my friends who are doctors: and the same and even more emphatic on behalf of all the painters, artists, and literary men with whom I have had the good fortune to be very closely associated. Of the clergy, I cannot speak. But in days more cheerful than the present gloomy times there were at least those of them who thought a glass of port no very dreadful sin.

And, conversely, I can say with all convinction that I have never seen drunken professors lecturing to inebriated students, or tipsy judges listening to boozy lawyers, or artists in delirium tremens painting the portraits of intoxicated Senators. Moreover, among the class of people of whom I speak, the conception of how to make merry at a christening or a wedding or a banquet or at the conclusion of peace, or of any such poor occasions of happiness that mark the milestones in the pilgrimage of life, was exactly the same – I say it in all reverence – as that shown by Jesus Christ at the wedding feast of Cana of Galilee.

But these people, one might object, are but a class, and a small one at that. What about the ordinary workingman? Surely he is not to be sacrificed for the sake of the leisure hours of the intellectual classes! But here, so it seems to me, is where the strongest argument against prohibition comes in. We live in a world of appalling inequality, which as yet neither philanthropy nor legislation has been able to remove. The lot of the workingman who begins day labor at the age of sixteen and ends it at the age of seventy, who starts work every morning while the rest of us are still in bed, who has no sleep after his lunch, and no vacation trip to Florida, is inconceivably hard. It is a sober fact that if those of us who are doctors, lawyers, professors, and merchants were suddenly transferred by some evil magician to the rank of a workingman, we should feel much as if we had been sent to the penitentiary. And it is equally a fact that we should realize just how much a glass of ale and a pipe of tobacco means to a sober industrious workingman – not a picture-book drunkard – after his hours of work. It puts him for the moment of his relaxation on an equality with kings and plutocrats.

It is no use to say that tobacco shortens his life. Let it. It needs shortening. It is no use to say that beer sogs his oesophagus and loosens his motor muscles. Let it do so. He is better off with loose motor muscles and a soggy oesophagus and a mug of ale beside him than in the cheerless discontent of an activity that knows only the work of life and nothing of its comforts.

The employers of labor have hitherto, through sheer short-sightedness, been in favor of prohibition. They thought that drink-less men would work better. So they will in the short spurt of efficiency that accompanies the change. But let the employer wait a year or two and then see how social discontent will spread like a wave in the wake of prohibition. The drinkless workman, robbed of the simple comforts of life, will angrily demand its luxuries. A new envy will enter into his heart. The glaring inequalities of society will stand revealed to him as never before. See to it that he does not turn into a Bolshevik.

For the fundamental fallacy of prohibition is that it proposes to make a crime of a thing which the conscience of the great mass of individuals refuses to consider as such. It violates here the principle on which, and on which alone, a criminal code can be based. If I steal another man's money, if I rob another man's house, if I take another man's life, I do not need the law to tell me that it is wrong. My own conscience tells me that. But if I take a glass of beer, my own conscience, in spite of all the laws of forty-eight states and nine provinces, refuses to give a single throb. Let me illustrate what I mean by an example.

A month or two ago I had the honor of being at a banquet given in the club to which I belong, to one of the most justly distinguished men of to-day – a certain vc who performed a certain naval exploit in bottling up (itself, by the way, an illegal act, had he done it in Canada) a certain harbor. Nearer than that I must not indicate him, inasmuch as I rather think that he is liable to a fine of two hundred dollars if the prohibitionists of Canada can catch him: unless I am mistaken, I saw somebody treat him to a whiskey and soda: and 'treating' and being 'treated' even in the present state of the law of the Province of Quebec is a crime.

Now the point I want to make is this. At the banquet of which I speak there were present a great number of the best-known men in Montreal: judges, lawyers, merchants, and men eminent in various walks of life. And everyone of them – or nearly everyone of them – was actually 'drinking something' with his dinner. Luckily for them the final law had not yet come into effect. If now they repeat their performance, they will be treated as in the same class as a group of burglars, or thugs, or yeggmen. To jail they must go. If they have no conscience of their own a substitute for it must be terrorized into them.

It is, of course, inevitable that a legislative code resting on so false a basis cannot last. Prohibition will not last forever. Sooner or later there will be a return to common sense and common justice. But the end will not come for a long time yet. Organized tyranny is difficult to break. Especially is this true of the United States, where an amendment to the Constitution once accepted requires for its removal an intricate and prolonged process of legislation. Without the war, national prohibition would never have been voted even by the politicians. It has swept through the Legislatures on a false wave of agitation masquerading as patriotism. It owed much to the fact that Germans are by way of drinking beer, and that such names as Anheuser Busch and Schlitz and Papst do not somehow sound altogether British. But as it came, so it will go. The unexpected will happen again. In the course of time some unforeseen contingency will send a new amendment rippling through the American Legislatures. Social life and individual liberty will be freed from the incubus that now lies on them.

Meanwhile, it is well for the British people to be warned. If they do not strangle in its cradle the snake of prohibition, then the country will be given over in its due time to the régime of the fanatic, the informer and the tyrant, such as we have in North America even now.

The unsolved riddle of social justice

1 The troubled outlook of the present hour

THESE ARE troubled times. As the echoes of the war die away the
sound of a new conflict rises on our ears. All the world is filled
with industrial unrest. Strike follows upon strike. A world that has
known five years of fighting has lost its taste for the honest
drudgery of work. Cincinnatus will not back to his plow, or, at
the best, stands sullenly between his plow-handles arguing for a
higher wage.

The wheels of industry are threatening to stop. The labourer will
not work because the pay is too low and the hours are too long. The
producer cannot employ him because the wage is too high, and the
hours are too short. If the high wage is paid and the short hours are
granted, then the price of the thing made, so it seems, rises higher
still. Even the high wages will not buy it. The process apparently
moves in a circle with no cessation to it. The increased wages seem
only to aggravate the increasing prices. Wages and prices, rising
together, call perpetually for more money, or at least more tokens
and symbols, more paper credit in the form of cheques and deposits,
with a value that is no longer based on the rock-bottom of redemp-
tion into hard coin, but that floats upon the mere atmosphere of
expectation.

But the sheer quantity of the inflated currency and false money
forces prices higher still. The familiar landmarks of wages, salaries
and prices are being obliterated. The 'scrap of paper' with which the
war began stays with us as its legacy. It lies upon the industrial
landscape like snow, covering up, as best it may, the bare poverty of
a world desolated by war.

Under such circumstances national finance seems turned into a
delirium. Billions are voted where once a few poor millions were
thought extravagant. The war debts of the Allied Nations, not yet
fully computed, will run from twenty-five to forty billion dollars
apiece. But the debts of the governments appear on the other side of
the ledger as the assets of the citizens. What is the meaning of it? Is
it wealth or is it poverty? The world seems filled with money and
short of goods, while even in this very scarcity a new luxury has
broken out. The capitalist rides in his ten thousand dollar motor car.
The seven-dollar-a-day artisan plays merrily on his gramophone in
the broad daylight of his afternoon that is saved, like all else, by
being 'borrowed' from the morning. He calls the capitalist a
'profiteer.' The capitalist retorts with calling him a 'Bolshevik.'

Worse portents appear. Over the rim of the Russian horizon are seen the fierce eyes and the unshorn face of the real and undoubted Bolshevik, waving his red flag. Vast areas of what was a fertile populated world are overwhelmed in chaos. Over Russia there lies a great darkness, spreading ominously westward into central Europe. The criminal sits among his corpses. He feeds upon the wreck of a civilization that was.

The infection spreads. All over the world the just claims of organized labour are intermingled with the underground conspiracy of social revolution. The public mind is confused. Something approaching to a social panic appears. To some minds the demand for law and order overwhelms all other thoughts. To others the fierce desire for social justice obliterates all fear of a general catastrophe. They push nearer and nearer to the brink of the abyss. The warning cry of 'back' is challenged by the eager shout of 'forward!' The older methods of social progress are abandoned as too slow. The older weapons of social defense are thrown aside as too blunt. Parliamentary discussion is powerless. It limps in the wake of the popular movement. The 'state,' as we knew it, threatens to dissolve into labour unions, conventions, boards of conciliation, and conferences. Society shaken to its base, hurls itself into the industrial suicide of the general strike, refusing to feed itself, denying its own wants.

This is a time such as there never was before. It represents a vast social transformation in which there is at stake, and may be lost, all that has been gained in the slow centuries of material progress and in which there may be achieved some part of all that has been dreamed in the age-long passion for social justice.

For the time being, the constituted governments of the world survive as best they may and accomplish such things as they can, planless, or planning at best only for the day. Sufficient, and more than sufficient, for the day is the evil thereof.

Never then was there a moment in which there was greater need for sane and serious thought. It is necessary to consider from the ground up the social organization in which we live and the means whereby it may be altered and expanded to meet the needs of the time to come. We must do this or perish. If we do not mend the machine, there are forces moving in the world that will break it. The blind Samson of labour will seize upon the pillars of society and bring them down in a common destruction.

Few persons can attain to adult life without being profoundly impressed by the appalling inequalities of our human lot. Riches and poverty jostle one another upon our streets. The tattered outcast dozes on his bench while the chariot of the wealthy is drawn by. The palace is the neighbour of the slum. We are, in modern life, so used to this that we no longer see it.

Inequality begins from the very cradle. Some are born into an easy and sheltered affluence. Others are the children of mean and sordid want. For some the long toil of life begins in the very bloom time of childhood and ends only when the broken and exhausted body sinks into a penurious old age. For others life is but a foolish leisure with mock activities and mimic avocations to mask its uselessness. And as the circumstances vary so too does the native endowment of the body and the mind. Some born in poverty rise to wealth. An inborn energy and capacity bid defiance to the ill-will of fate. Others sink. The careless hand lets fall the cradle gift of wealth.

Thus all about us is the moving and shifting spectacle of riches and poverty, side by side, inextricable.

The human mind, lost in a maze of inequalities that it cannot explain and evils that it cannot, singly, remedy, must adapt itself as best it can. An acquired indifference to the ills of others is the price at which we live. A certain dole of sympathy, a casual mite of personal relief is the mere drop that any one of us alone can cast into the vast ocean of human misery. Beyond that we must harden ourselves lest we too perish. We feed well while others starve. We make fast the doors of our lighted houses against the indigent and the hungry. What else can we do? If we shelter *one* what is that? And if we try to shelter all, we are ourselves shelterless.

But the contrast thus presented is one that has acquired a new meaning in the age in which we live. The poverty of earlier days was the outcome of the insufficiency of human labour to meet the primal needs of human kind. It is not so now. We live in an age that is at best about a century and a half old — the age of machinery and power. Our common reading of history has obscured this fact. Its pages are filled with the purple gowns of kings and the scarlet trappings of the warrior. Its record is largely that of battles and sieges, of the brave adventure of discovery and the vexed slaughter of the nations. It has long since dismissed as too short and simple for its pages, the short and simple annals of the poor. And the record is right enough. Of the poor what is there to say? They were born; they lived; they died. They followed their leaders, and their names are forgotten.

But written thus our history has obscured the greatest fact that ever came into it — the colossal change that separates our little era of a century and a half from all the preceding history of mankind — separates it so completely that a great gulf lies between, across which comparison can scarcely pass, and on the other side of which a new world begins.

It has been the custom of our history to use the phrase the 'new world' to mark the discoveries of Columbus and the treasure-hunt of a Cortes or a Pizarro. But what of that? The America that they annexed to Europe was merely a new domain added to a world already old. The 'new world' was really found in the wonder-years of the eighteenth and early nineteenth centuries. Mankind really entered upon it when the sudden progress of liberated science bound the fierce energy of expanding stream and drew the eager lightning from the cloud.

Here began indeed, in the drab surroundings of the workshop, in the silent mystery of the laboratory, the magic of the new age.

But we do not commonly realize the vastness of the change. Much of our life and much of our thought still belongs to the old world. Our education is still largely framed on the old pattern. And our views of poverty and social betterment, or what is possible and what is not, are still largely conditioned by it.

In the old world, poverty seemed, and poverty was, the natural and inevitable lot of the greater portion of mankind. It was difficult, with the mean appliances of the time, to wring subsistence from the reluctant earth. For the simplest necessaries and comforts of life all, or nearly all, must work hard. Many must perish for want of them. Poverty was inevitable and perpetual. The poor must look to the brightness of a future world for the consolation that they were denied in this. Seen thus poverty became rather a blessing than a curse, or at least a dispensation prescribing the proper lot of man. Life itself was but a preparation and a trial — a threshing floor where, under the 'tribulation' of want, the wheat was beaten from the straw. Of this older view much still survives, and much that is ennobling. Nor is there any need to say good-by to it. Even if poverty were gone, the flail could still beat hard enough upon the grain and chaff of humanity.

But turn to consider the magnitude of the change that has come about with the era of machinery and the indescribable increase which it has brought to man's power over his environment. There is no need to recite here in detail the marvelous record of mechanical progress that constituted the 'industrial revolution' of the eighteenth century. The utilization of coal for the smelting of iron ore; the invention of machinery that could spin and weave; the application of the undreamed energy of steam as a motive force, the building of canals and the making of stone roads — these proved but the beginnings. Each stage of invention called for a further advance. The quickening of one part of the process necessitated the 'speeding up' of all the others. It placed a premium — a reward already in sight — upon the next advance. Mechanical spinning called forth the power loom. The increase in production called for new means of transport. The improvement of transport still further swelled the volume of production. The steamboat of 1809 and the steam locomotive of 1830 were the direct result of what had gone before. Most important of all, the movement had become a conscious one. Invention was no longer the fortuitous result of a happy chance. Mechanical progress, the continual increase of power and the continual surplus of product became an essential part of the environment, and an unconscious element in the thought and outlook of the civilized world.

No wonder that the first aspect of the age of machinery was one of triumph. Man had vanquished nature. The elemental forces of wind and fire, of rushing water and driving storm before which the savage had cowered low for shelter, these had become his servants. The forest that had blocked his path became his field. The desert blossomed as his garden.

The aspect of industrial life altered. The domestic industry of the cottage and the individual labour of the artisan gave place to the factory with its regiment of workers and its steam-driven machinery. The economic isolation of the single worker, of the village, even of the district and the nation, was lost in the general cohesion in which the whole industrial world merged into one.

The life of the individual changed accordingly. In the old world his little sphere was allotted to him and there he stayed. His village was his horizon. The son of the weaver wove and the smith reared his children to his trade. Each did his duty, or was adjured to do it, in the 'state of life to which it had pleased God to call him.' Migration to distant occupations or to foreign lands was but for the adventurous few. The ne'er-do-well blew, like seed before the wind, to distant places, but mankind at large stayed at home. Here and there exceptional industry or extraordinary capacity raised the artisan to wealth and turned the 'man' into the 'master.' But for the most part even industry and endowment were powerless against the inertia of custom and the dead-weight of environment. The universal ignorance of the working class broke down the aspiring force of genius. Mute inglorious Miltons were buried in country churchyards.

In the new world all this changed. The individual became but a shifting atom in the vast complex, moving from place to place, from occupation to occupation and from gradation to gradation of material fortune.

The process went further and further. The machine penetrated everywhere, thrusting aside with its gigantic arm the feeble efforts of handicraft. It laid its hold upon agriculture, sowing and reaping the grain and transporting it to the ends of the earth. Then as the nineteenth century drew towards its close, even the age of steam power was made commonplace by achievements of the era of electricity.

All this is familiar enough. The record of the age of machinery is known to all. But the strange mystery, the secret that lies concealed within its organization, is realized by but few. It offers, to those who see it aright, the most perplexing industrial paradox ever presented in the history of mankind. With all our wealth, we are still poor. After a century and a half of labour-saving machinery, we work about as hard as ever. With a power over nature multiplied a hundred fold, nature still conquers us. And more than this. There are many senses in which the machine age seems to leave the great bulk of civilized humanity, the working part of it, worse off instead of better. The nature of our work has changed. No man now makes anything. He makes only a part of something, feeding and tending a machine that moves with relentless monotony in the routine of which both the machine and its tender are only a fractional part.

For the great majority of the workers, the interest of work as such is gone. It is a task done consciously for a wage, one eye upon the clock. The brave independence of the keeper of the little shop contrasts favourably with the mock dignity of a floor walker in an 'establishment.' The varied craftsmanship of the artisan had in it something of the creative element that was the parent motive of sustained industry. The dull routine of the factory hand in a cotton mill has gone. The life of a pioneer settler in America two hundred years ago, penurious and dangerous as it was, stands out brightly beside the dull and meaningless toil of his descendant.

The picture must not be drawn in colours too sinister. In the dullest work and in the meanest lives in the new world to-day there are elements that were lacking in the work of the old world. The universal spread of elementary education, the universal access to the printed page, and the universal hope of better things, if not for oneself, at least for one's children, and even the universal restlessness that the industrialism of to-day have brought are better things than the dull plodding passivity of the older world. Only a false mediae-valism can paint the past in colours superior to the present. The haze of distance that dims the mountains with purple, shifts also the crude colours of the past into the soft glory of retrospect. Misled by these, the sentimentalist may often sigh for an age that in a nearer view would be seen filled with cruelty and suffering. But even when we have made every allowance for the all too human tendency to soften down the past, it remains true that in many senses the pro-cesses of industry for the worker have lost in attractiveness and power of absorption of the mind during the very period when they have gained so enormously in effectiveness and in power of production.

The essential contrast lies between the vastly increased power of production and its apparent inability to satisfy for all humanity the most elementary human wants; between the immeasurable saving of labour effected by machinery and the brute fact of the continuance of hard-driven, unceasing toil.

Of the extent of this increased power of production we can only speak in general terms. No one, as far as I am aware, has yet essayed to measure it. Nor have we any form of calculus or computation that can easily be applied. If we wish to compare the gross total of production effected to-day with that accomplished a hundred and fifty years ago, the means, the basis of calculation, is lacking. Vast numbers of the things produced now were not then in existence. A great part of our production of to-day culminates not in productive goods, but in services as in forms of motion, or in ability to talk across a distance.

It is true that statistics that deal with the world's production of cotton, or of oil, or of iron and steel present stupendous results. But even these do not go far enough. For the basic raw materials are worked into finer and finer forms to supply new 'wants' as they are called, and to represent a vast quantity of 'satisfactions' not existing before.

Nor is the money calculus of any avail. Comparison by prices breaks down entirely. A bushel of wheat stands about where it stood before and could be calculated. But the computation, let us say, in price-values of the Sunday newspapers produced in one week in New York or the annual output of photographic apparatus, would defy comparison. Of the enormous increase in the gross total of human goods there is no doubt. We have only to look about us to see it. The endless miles of railways, the vast apparatus of the factories, the soaring structures of the cities bear easy witness to it. Yet it would be difficult indeed to compute by what factor the effectiveness of human labour working with machinery has been increased.

But suppose we say, since one figure is as good as another, that it has been increased a hundred times. This calculation must be well within the facts and can be used as merely a more concrete way of saying that the power of production has been vastly increased. During the period of this increase, the numbers of mankind in the industrial countries have perhaps been multiplied by three to one. This again is inexact, since there are no precise figures of population that cover the period. But all that is meant is that the increase in one case is, quite obviously, colossal, and in the other case is evidently not very much.

Here then is the paradox.

If the ability to produce goods to meet human wants has multiplied so that each man accomplishes almost thirty or forty times what he did before, then the world at large ought to be about thirty of fifty times better of. But it is not. Or else, as the other possible alternative, the working hours of the world should have been cut down to about one in thirty of what they were before. But they are not. How, then, are we to explain this extraordinary discrepancy between human power and resulting human happiness?

The more we look at our mechanism of production the more perplexing it seems. Suppose an observer were to look down from the cold distance of the moon upon the seething ant-hill of human labour presented on the surface of our globe; and suppose that such an observer knew nothing of our system of individual property, of money payments and wages and contracts, but viewed our labour as merely that of a mass of animated beings trying to supply their wants. The spectacle to his eyes would be strange indeed. Mankind viewed in the mass would be seen to produce a certain amount of absolutely necessary things, such as food, and then to stop. In spite of the fact that there was not food enough to go round, and that large numbers must die of starvation or perish slowly from under-nutrition, the production of food would stop at some point a good deal short of universal satisfaction. So, too, with the production of clothing, shelter and other necessary things; never enough would seem to be produced, and this apparently not by accident or mis-calculation, but as if some peculiar social law were at work adjusting production to the point where there is just not enough, and leaving it there. The countless millions of workers would be seen to turn their untired energies and their all-powerful machinery away from the production of necessary things to the making of mere comforts; and from these, again, while still stopping short of a general satis-faction, to the making of luxuries and superfluities. The wheels would never stop. The activity would never tire. Mankind, mad with the energy of activity, would be seen to pursue the fleeing phantom of insatiable desire. Thus among the huge mass of accumulated commodities the simplest wants would go unsatisfied. Half-fed men would dig for diamonds, and men sheltered by a crazy roof erect the marble walls of palaces. The observer might well remain perplexed at the pathetic discord between human work and human wants. Some-thing, he would feel assured, must be at fault either with the social instincts of man or with the social order under which he lives.

And herein lies the supreme problem that faces us in this opening century. The period of five years of war has shown it to us in a clearer light than fifty years of peace. War is destruction – the annihilation of human life, the destruction of things made with generations of labour, the misdirection of productive power from making what is useful to making what is useless. In the great war just over, some seven million lives were sacrificed; eight million tons of shipping were sunk beneath the sea; some fifty million adult males were drawn from productive labour to the lines of battle; behind them uncounted millions laboured day and night at making the weapons of destruction. One might well have thought that such a gigantic misdirection of human energy would have brought the industrial world to a standstill within a year. So people did think. So thought a great number, perhaps the greater number, of the financiers and economists and industrial leaders trained in the world in which we used to live. The expectation was unfounded. Great as is the destruction of war, not even five years of it have broken the productive machine. And the reason is now plain enough. Peace, also – or peace under the old conditions of industry – is infinitely wasteful of human energy. Not more than one adult worker in ten – so a leading American economist has declared – is employed on necessary things. The other nine perform superfluous services. War turns them from making the glittering superfluities of peace to making its grim engines of destruction. But while the tenth man still labours, the machine, though creaking with its dislocation, can still go on. The economics of war, therefore, has thrown its lurid light upon the economics of peace.

These I propose in the succeeding chapters to examine. But it might be well before doing so to lay stress upon the fact that while admitting all the shortcomings and the injustices of the régime under which we have lived, I am not one of those who are able to see a short and single remedy. Many people when presented with the argument above, would settle it at once with the word 'socialism.' Here, they say, is the immediate and natural remedy. I confess at the outset, and shall develop later, that I cannot view it so. Socialism is a mere beautiful dream, possible only for the angels. The attempt to establish it would hurl us over the abyss. Our present lot is sad, but the frying pan is at least better than the fire.

2 Life, liberty, and the pursuit of happiness

'ALL MEN,' wrote Thomas Jefferson in framing the Declaration of Independence, 'have an inalienable right to life, liberty and the pursuit of happiness.' The words are more than a felicitous phrase. They express even more than the creed of a nation. They embody in themselves the uppermost thought of the era that was dawning when they were written. They stand for the same view of society which, in that very year of 1776, Adam Smith put before the world in his immortal 'Wealth of Nations' as the 'System of Natural Liberty,' In this system mankind placed its hopes for over half a century and under it the industrial civilization of the age of machinery rose to the plenitude of its power.

In the preceding chapter an examination has been made of the purely mechanical side of the era of machine production. It has been shown that the age of machinery has been in a certain sense one of triumph, of the triumphant conquest of nature, but in another sense one of perplexing failure. The new forces controlled by mankind have been powerless as yet to remove want and destitution, hard work and social discontent. In the midst of accumulated wealth social justice seems as far away as ever.

It remains now to discuss the intellectual development of the modern age of machinery and the way in which it has moulded the thoughts and the outlook of mankind.

Few men think for themselves. The thoughts of most of us are little more than imitations and adaptations of the ideas of stronger minds. The influence of environment conditions, if it does not control, the mind of man. So it comes about that every age or generation has its dominant and uppermost thoughts, its peculiar way of looking at things and its peculiar basis of opinion on which its collective action and its social regulations rest. All this is largely unconscious. The average citizen of three generations ago was probably not aware that he was an extreme individualist. The average citizen of to-day is not conscious of the fact that he has ceased to be one. The man of three generations ago had certain ideas which he held to be axiomatic, such as that his house was his castle, and that property was property and that what was his was his. But these were to him things so obvious that he could not conceive any reasonable person doubting them. So, too, with the man of to-day. He has come to believe in such things as old age pensions and national insurance. He submits to bachelor taxes and he pays for the education of other people's children; he speculates much on the limits of inheritance, and he even meditates profound alterations in the right of property in land. His house is no longer his castle. He has taken down its fences, and 'boulevarded' its grounds till it merges into those of his neighbours. Indeed he probably does not live in a house at all, but in a mere 'apartment' or subdivision of a house which he shares with a multiplicity of people. Nor does he any longer draw water from his own well or go to bed by the light of his own candle: for such services as these his life is so mixed up with 'franchises' and 'public utilities' and other things unheard of by his own great-grandfather, that it is hopelessly intertangled with that of his fellow citizens. In fine, there is little left but his own conscience into which he can withdraw.

Such a man is well aware that times have changed since his great-grandfather's day. But he is not aware of the profound extent to which his own opinions have been affected by the changing times. He is no longer an individualist. He has become by brute force of circumstances a sort of collectivist, puzzled only as to how much of a collectivist to be.

Individualism of the extreme type is, therefore, long since out of date. To attack it is merely to kick a dead dog. But the essential problem of to-day is to know how far we are to depart from its principles. There are those who tell us – and they number many millions – that we must abandon them entirely. Industrial society, they say, must be reorganized from top to bottom; private industry must cease. All must work for the state; only in a socialist common-wealth can social justice be found. There are others, of whom the present writer is one, who see in such a programme nothing but disaster: yet who consider that the individualist principle of 'every man for himself' while it makes for national wealth and accumulated power, favours overmuch the few at the expense of the many, puts an over-great premium upon capacity, assigns too harsh a punish-ment for easy indolence, and, what is worse, exposes the individual human being too cruelly to the mere accidents of birth and fortune. Under such a system, in short, to those who have is given and from those who have not is taken away even that which they have. There are others again who still view individualism just as the vast majority of our great-grandfathers viewed it, as a system hard but just: as awarding to every man the fruit of his own labour and the punishment of his own idleness, and as visiting, in accordance with the stern but necessary ordination of our existence, the sins of the father upon the child.

The proper starting point, then, for all discussion of the social problem is the consideration of the individualist theory of industrial society. This grew up, as all the world knows, along with the era of machinery itself. It had its counterpart on the political side in the rise of representative democratic government. Machinery, industrial liberty, political democracy – these three things represent the basis of the progress of the nineteenth century.

The chief exposition of the system is found in the work of the classical economists – Adam Smith and his followers of half a century – who created the modern science of political economy. Beginning as controversialists anxious to overset a particular system of trade regulation, they ended by becoming the exponents of a new social order. Modified and amended as their system is in its practical application, it still largely conditions our outlook to-day. It is to this system that we must turn.

The general outline of the classical theory of political economy is so clear and so simple that it can be presented within the briefest compass. It began with certain postulates, or assumptions, to a great extent unconscious, of the conditions to which it applied. It assumed the existence of the state and of contract. It took for granted the existence of individual property, in consumption goods, in capital goods, and, with a certain hesitation, in land. The last assumption was not perhaps without misgivings: Adam Smith was disposed to look askance at landlords as men who gathered where they had not sown. John Stuart Mill, as is well known, was more and more inclined, with advancing reflection, to question the sanctity of landed property as the basis of social institutions. But for the most part property, contract and the coercive state were fundamental assumptions with the classicists.

With this there went, on the psychological side, the further assumption of a general selfishness or self-seeking as the principal motive of the individual in the economic sphere. Oddly enough this assumption – the most warrantable of the lot – was the earliest to fall under disrepute. The plain assertion that every man looks out for himself (or at best for himself and his immediate family) touches the tender conscience of humanity. It is an unpalatable truth. None the less it is the most nearly true of all the broad generalizations that can be attempted in regard to mankind.

The essential problem then of the classicists was to ask what would happen if an industrial community, possessed of the modern control over machinery and power, were allowed to follow the promptings of 'enlightened selfishness' in an environment based upon free contract and the right of property in land and goods. The answer was of the most cheering description. The result would be a progressive amelioration of society, increasing in proportion to the completeness with which the fundamental principles involved were allowed to act, and tending ultimately towards something like a social millenium or perfection of human society. One easily recalls the almost reverent attitude of Adam Smith towards this system of industrial liberty which he exalted into a kind of natural theology: and the way in which Mill, a deist but not a Christian, was able to fit the whole apparatus of individual liberty into its place in an ordered universe. The world 'runs of itself,' said the economist. We have only to leave it alone. And the maxim of *laissez-faire* became the last word of social wisdom.

The argument of the classicists ran thus. If there is everywhere complete economic freedom, then there will ensue in consequence a régime of social justice. If every man is allowed to buy and sell goods, labour and property, just as suits his own interest, then the prices and wages that result are either in the exact measure of social justice or, at least, are perpetually moving towards it. The price of any commodity at any moment is, it is true, a 'market price,' the resultant of the demand and the supply; but behind this operates continually the inexorable law of the cost of production. Sooner or later every price must represent the actual cost of producing the commodity concerned, or, at least, must oscillate now above and now below that point which it is always endeavoring to meet. For if temporary circumstances force the price well above the cost of producing the article in question, then the large profits to be made induce a greater and greater production. The increased volume of the supply thus produced inevitably forces down the price till it sinks to the point of cost. If circumstances (such, for example, as miscalculation and an over-great supply) depress the price below the point of cost, then the discouragement of further production presently shortens the supply and brings the price up again. Price is thus like an oscillating pendulum seeking its point of rest, or like the waves of the sea rising and falling about its level. By this same mechanism the quantity and direction of production, argued the economists, respond automatically to the needs of humanity, or, at least, to the 'effective demand,' which the classicist mistook for the same thing. Just as much wheat or bricks or diamonds would be produced as the world called for; to produce too much of any one thing was to violate a natural law; the falling price and the resulting temporary loss sternly rebuked the producer.

In the same way the technical form and mechanism of production were presumed to respond to an automatic stimulus. Inventions and improved processes met their own reward. Labour, so it was argued, was perpetually being saved by the constant introduction of new uses of machinery.

By a parity of reasoning, the shares received by all the participants and claimants in the general process of production were seen to be regulated in accordance with natural law. Interest on capital was treated merely as a particular case under the general theory of price. It was the purchase price needed to call forth the 'saving' (a form, so to speak, of production) which brought the capital into the market. The 'profits' of the employer represented the necessary price paid by society for his services, just enough and not more than enough to keep him and his fellows in operative activity, and always tending under the happy operation of competition to fall to the minimum consistent with social progress.

Rent, the share of the land-owner, offered to the classicist a rather peculiar case. There was here a physical basis of surplus over cost. But, granted the operation of the factors and forces concerned, rent emerged as a differential payment to the fortunate owner of the soil. It did not in any way affect prices or wages, which were rendered neither greater nor less thereby. The full implication of the rent doctrine and its relation to social justice remained obscured to the eye of the classical economist; the fixed conviction that what a man owns is his own created a mist through which the light could not pass.

Wages, finally, were but a further case of value. There was a demand for labour, represented by the capital waiting to remunerate it, and a supply of labour represented by the existing and increasing working class. Hence wages, like all other shares and factors, corresponded, so it was argued, to social justice. Whether wages were high or low, whether hours were long or short, at least the labourer like everybody else 'got what was coming to him.' All possibility of a general increase of wages depended on the relation of available capital to the numbers of the working men.

Thus the system as applied to society at large could be summed up in the consoling doctrine that every man got what he was worth, and was worth what he got; that industry and energy brought their own reward; that national wealth and individual welfare were one and the same; that all that was needed for social progress was hard work, more machinery, more saving of labour and a prudent limitation of the numbers of the population.

The application of such a system to legislation and public policy was obvious. It carried with it the principle of *laissez-faire*. The doctrine of international free trade, albeit the most conspicuous of its applications, was but one case under the general law. It taught that the mere organization of labour was powerless to raise wages; that strikes were of no avail, or could at best put a shilling into the pocket of one artisan by taking it out of that of another; that wages and prices could not be regulated by law; that poverty was to a large extent a biological phenomenon representing the fierce struggle of germinating life against the environment that throttles part of it. The poor were like the fringe of grass that fades or dies where it meets the sand of the desert. There could be no social remedy for poverty except the almost impossible remedy of the limitation of life itself. Failing this the economist could wash his hands of the poor.

These are the days of relative judgments and the classical economy, like all else, must be viewed in the light of time and circumstance. With all its fallacies, or rather its shortcomings, it served a magnificent purpose. It opened a road never before trodden from social slavery towards social freedom, from the mediaeval autocratic régime of fixed caste and hereditary status towards a régime of equal social justice. In this sense the classical economy was but the fruition, or rather represented the final consciousness of a process that had been going on for centuries, since the breakdown of feudalism and the emancipation of the serf. True, the goal has not been reached. The vision of the universal happiness seen by the economists has proved a mirage. The end of the road is not in sight. But it cannot be doubted that in the long pilgrimage of mankind towards social betterment the economists guided us in the right turning. If we turn again in a new direction, it will at any rate not be in the direction of a return to autocratic mediaevalism.

But when all is said in favour of its historic usefulness, the failures and the fallacies of natural liberty have now become so manifest that the system is destined in the coming era to be revised from top to bottom. It is to these failures and fallacies that attention will be drawn in the next chapter.

3 The failures and fallacies of natural liberty

THE REWARDS and punishments of the economic world are singularly unequal. One man earns as much in a week or even in a day as
another does in a year. This man by hard, manual labour makes only
enough to pay for humble shelter and plain food. This other by what
seems a congenial activity, fascinating as a game of chess, acquires
uncounted millions. A third stands idle in the market place asking in
vain for work. A fourth lives upon rent, dozing in his chair, and
neither toils nor spins. A fifth by the sheer hazard of a lucky 'deal'
acquires a fortune without work at all. A sixth, scorning to work,
earns nothing and gets nothing; in him survives a primitive dislike of
labour not yet fully 'evoluted out'; he slips through the meshes of
civilization to become a 'tramp,' cadges his food where he can, suns
his tattered rags when it is warm and shivers when it is cold, migrat-
ing with the birds and reappearing with the flowers of spring.

Yet all are free. This is the distinguishing mark of them as children of our era. They may work or stop. There is no compulsion
from without. No man is a slave. Each has his 'natural liberty,' and
each in his degree, great or small, receives his allotted reward.

But is the allotment correct and the reward proportioned by his
efforts? Is it fair or unfair, and does it stand for the true measure of
social justice?

This is the profound problem of the twentieth century.

The economists and the leading thinkers of the nineteenth
century were in no doubt about this question. It was their firm
conviction that the system under which we live was, in its broad
outline, a system of even justice. They held it true that every man
under free competition and individual liberty is awarded just what
he is worth and is worth exactly what he gets: that the reason why a
plain labourer is paid only two or three dollars a day is because he
only 'produces' two or three dollars a day: and that why a skilled
engineer is paid ten times as much is because he 'produces' ten times
as much. His work is 'worth' ten times that of the plain labourer. By
the same reasoning the salary of a corporation president who
receives fifty thousand dollars a year merely reflects the fact that the
man produces — earns — brings in to the corporation that amount or
even more. The big salary corresponds to the big efficiency.

And there is much in the common experience of life and the
common conduct of business that seems to support this view. It is
undoubtedly true if we look at any little portion of business activity

taken as a fragment by itself. On the most purely selfish grounds I may find that it 'pays' to hire an expert at a hundred dollars a day, and might find that it spelled ruin to attempt to raise the wages of my working men beyond four dollars a day. Everybody knows that in any particular business at any particular place and time with prices at any particular point, there is a wage that can be paid and a wage that can not. And everybody, or nearly everybody, bases on these obvious facts a series of entirely erroneous conclusions. Because we cannot change the part we are apt to think we cannot change the whole. Because one brick in the wall is immovable, we forget that the wall itself might be rebuilt.

The single employer rightly knows that there is a wage higher than he can pay and hours shorter than he can grant. But are the limits that frame him in, real and necessary limits, resulting from the very nature of things, or are they mere products of particular circumstances? This, as a piece of pure economics, does not interest the individual employer a particle. It belongs in the same category as the question of the immortality of the soul and other profundities that have nothing to do with business. But to society at large the question is of an infinite importance.

Now the older economists taught, and the educated world for about a century believed, that these limitations which hedged the particular employer about were fixed and assigned by natural economic law. They represented, as has been explained, the operation of the system of natural liberty by which every man got what he is worth. And it is quite true that the particular employer can no more break away from these limits than he can jump out of his own skin. He can only violate them at the expense of ceasing to be an economic being at all and degenerating into a philanthropist.

But consider for a moment the peculiar nature of the limitations themselves. Every man's limit of what he can pay and what he can take, of how much he can offer and how much he will receive, is based on the similar limitations of other people. They are reciprocal to one another. Why should one factory owner not pay ten dollars a day to his hands? Because the others don't. But suppose they all do? Then the output could not be sold at the present price. But why not sell the produce at a higher price? Because at a higher price the consumer can't afford to buy it. But suppose that the consumer, for the things which he himself makes and sells, or for the work which

he performs, receives more? What then? The whole thing begins to
have a jigsaw look, like a child's toy rack with wooden soldiers on it,
expanding and contracting. One searches in vain for the basis on
which the relationship rests. And at the end of the analysis one finds
nothing but a mere anarchical play of forces, nothing but a give-and-
take resting on relative bargaining strength. Every man gets what he
can and gives what he has to.

Observe that this is not in the slightest the conclusion of the
orthodox economists. Every man, they said, gets what he actually
makes, or, by exchange, those things which exactly correspond to it
as regards the cost of making them – which have, to use the key-
word of the theory, the same value. Let us take a very simple
example. If I go fishing with a net which I have myself constructed
out of fibers and sticks, and if I catch a fish and if I then roast the
fish over a fire which I have made without so much as the inter-
vention of a lucifer match, then it is I and I alone who have 'produced' the roast fish. That is plain enough. But what if I catch the
fish by using a hired boat and a hired net, or by buying worms as
bait from some one who has dug them? Or what if I do not fish at
all, but get my roast fish by paying for it a part of the wages I
receive for working in a saw mill? Here are a new set of relationships.
How much of the fish is 'produced' by each of the people concerned? And what part of my wages ought I to pay in return for the
part of the fish that I buy?

Here opens up, very evidently, a perfect labyrinth of complexity.
But it was the labyrinth for which the earlier economist held, so he
thought, the thread. No matter how dark the passage, he still clung
tight to it. And his thread was his 'fundamental equation of value'
whereby each thing and everything is sold (or tends to be sold)
under free competition for exactly its cost of production. There it
was; as simple as ABC; making the cost of everything proportional to
the cost of everything else, and in itself natural and just; explaining
and justifying the variations of wages and salaries on what seems a
stern basis of fact. Here is your selling price as a starting point. Given
that, you can see at once the reason for the wages paid and the full
measure of the payment. To pay more is impossible. To pay less is to
invite a competition that will force the payment of more. Or take, if
you like, the wages as the starting point: there you are

again — simplicity itself: the selling price will exactly and nicely correspond to cost. True, a part of the cost concerned will be represented not by wages, but by cost of materials; but these, on analysis, dissolve into past wages. Hence the whole process and its explanation revolves around this simple fundamental equation that selling value equals the cost of production.

This was the central part of the economic structure. It was the keystone of the arch. If it holds, all holds. Knock it out and the whole edifice falls into fragments.

A technical student of the schools would digress here, to the great confusion of the reader, into a discussion of the controversy in the economic cloister between the rival schools of economists as to whether cost governs value or value governs cost. The point needs no discussion here, but just such fleeting passing mention as may indicate that the writer is well and wearily conversant with it.

The fundamental equation of the economist, then, is that the value of everything is proportionate to its cost. It requires no little hardihood to say that this proposition is a fallacy. It lays one open at once, most illogically, to the charge of being a socialist. In sober truth it might as well lay one open to the charge of being an ornithologist. I will not, therefore, say that the proposition that the value of everything equals the cost of production is false. I will say that it is *true;* in fact, that is just as true as that two and two make four: exactly as true as that, but let it be noted most profoundly, *only as true as that.* In other words, it is a truism, mere equation in terms, telling nothing whatever. When I say that two and two make four I find, after deep thought, that I have really said *nothing,* or nothing that was not already said at the moment I defined two and defined four. The new statement that two and two make four adds nothing. So with the majestic equation of the cost of production. It means, as far as social application goes, as far as any moral significance or bearing on social reform and the social outlook goes, *absolutely nothing.* It is not in itself fallacious; how could it be? But all the social inferences drawn from it are absolute, complete and malicious fallacies.

Any socialist who says this, is quite right. Where he goes wrong is when he tries to build up as truth a set of inferences more fallacious and more malicious still.

But the central economic doctrine of cost can not be shaken by mere denunciation. Let us examine it and see what is the matter with it. We restate the equation.

Under perfectly free competition the value or selling price of everything equals, or is perpetually tending to equal, the cost of its production. This is the proposition itself, and the inferences derived from it are that there is a 'natural price' of everything, and that all 'natural prices' are proportionate to cost and to one another; that all wages, apart from temporary fluctuations, are derived from, and limited by, the natural prices paid for the things made: that all payments for the use of capital (interest) are similarly derived and similarly limited; and that consequently the whole economic arrangement, by giving to each person exactly and precisely the fruit of his own labour, conforms exactly to social justice.

Now the trouble with the main proposition just quoted is that each side of the equation is used as the measure of the other. In order to show what natural price is, we add up all the wages that have been paid, and declare that to be the cost and then say that the cost governs the price. Then if we are asked why are wages what they are, we turn the argument backward and say that since the selling price is so and so the wages that can be paid out of it only amount to such and such. This explains nothing. It is a mere argument in a circle. It is as if one tried to explain why one blade of a pair of scissors is four inches long by saying that it has to be the same length as the other. This is quite true of either blade if one takes the length of the other for granted, but as applied to the explanation of the length of the scissors it is worse than meaningless.

This reasoning may seem to many persons mere casuistry, mere sophistical juggling with words. After all, they say, there is such a thing as relative cost, relative difficulty of making things, a difference which rests upon a physical basis. To make one thing requires a lot of labour and trouble and much skill: to make another thing requires very little labour and no skill out of the common. Here then is your basis of value, obvious and beyond argument. A primitive savage makes a bow and arrow in a day: it takes him a fortnight to make a bark canoe. On that fact rests the exchange value between the two. The relative quantity of labour embodied in each object is the basis of its value.

This line of reasoning has a very convincing sound. It appears in nearly every book on economic theory from Adam Smith and Ricardo till to-day. 'Labour alone,' wrote Smith, 'never varying in its own value is above the ultimate and real standard by which the value of all commodities can at all times and places be estimated and compared.'

But the idea that *quantity of labour governs* value will not stand examination for a moment. What is *quantity* of labour and how is it measured? As long as we draw our illustrations from primitive life where one man's work is much the same as another's and where all operations are simple, we seem easily able to measure and compare. One day is the same as another and one man about as capable as his fellow. But in the complexity of modern industrial life such a calculation no longer applies: the differences of skill, of native ingenuity, and technical preparation become enormous. The hour's work of a common labourer is not the same thing as the hour's work of a watchmaker mending a watch, or of an engineer directing the building of a bridge, or of an architect drawing a plan. There is no way of reducing these hours to a common basis. We may think, if we like, that the quantity of labour *ought* to be the basis of value and exchange. Such is always the dream of the socialist. But on a closer view it is shattered like any other dream. For we have, alas, no means of finding out what the quantity of labour is and how it can be measured. We cannot measure it in terms of time. We have no calculus for comparing relative amounts of skill and energy. We cannot measure it by the amount of its contribution to the product, for that is the very matter that we want to discover.

What the economist does is to slip out of the difficulty altogether by begging the whole question. He deliberately measures the quantity of labour *by what is paid for it.* Skilled labour is worth, let us say, three times as much as common labour; and brain work, speaking broadly, is worth several times as much again. Hence by adding up all the wages and salaries paid we get something that seems to indicate the total quantity of labour, measured not simply in time, but with an allowance for skill and technical competency. By describing this allowance as a coefficient we can give our statement a false air of mathematical certainty and so muddle up the essential question that the truth is lost from sight like a pea under a thimble. Now you see it and now you don't. The thing is, in fact, a mere piece of intellectual conjuring. The conjurer has slipped the phrase, 'quantity of labour,' up his sleeve, and when it reappears it has turned into 'the expense of hiring labour.' This is a quite different thing. But as both conceptions are related somehow to the idea of cost, the substitution is never discovered.

On this false basis a vast structure is erected. All prices, provided that competition is free, are made to appear as the necessary result of natural forces. They are 'natural' or 'normal' prices. All wages are explained, and low wages are exonerated, on what seems to be an undeniable ground of fact. They are what they are. You may wish them otherwise, but they are not. As a philanthropist, you may feel sorry that a humble labourer should work through a long day to receive two dollars, but as an economist you console yourself with the reflection that that is all he produces. You may at times, as a sentimentalist, wonder whether the vast sums drawn as interest on capital are consistent with social fairness; but if it is shown that interest is simply the 'natural price' of capital representing the actual 'productive power' of the capital, there is nothing further to say. You may have similar qualms over rent and the rightness and wrongness of it. The enormous 'unearned increment' that accrues for the fortunate owner of land who toils not neither spins to obtain it, may seem difficult of justification. But after all, land is only one particular case of ownership under the one and the same system. The rent for which the owner can lease it, emerges simply as a consequence of the existing state of wages and prices. High rent, says the economist, does not make big prices: it merely follows as a consequence or result of them. Dear bread is not caused by the high rents paid by tenant farmers for the land: the train of cause and effect runs in the contrary direction. And the selling price of land is merely a consequence of its rental value, a simple case of capitalization of annual return into a present sum. City land, though it looks different from farm land, is seen in the light of this same analysis, to earn its rent in just the same way. The high rent of a Broadway store, says the economist, does not add a single cent to the price of the things sold in it. It is because prices are what they are that the rent is and can be paid. Hence on examination the same canon of social justice that covers and explains prices, wages, and interest applies with perfect propriety to rent.

Or finally, to take the strongest case of all, one may, as a citizen, feel apprehension at times at the colossal fortune of a Carnegie or a Rockefeller. For it does seem passing strange that one human being should control as property the mass of coin, goods, houses, factories, land and mines, represented by a billion dollars; stranger still that at his death he should write upon a piece of paper his commands as to what his surviving fellow creatures are to do with it. But if it can be shown to be true that Mr Rockefeller 'made' his fortune in the same sense that a man makes a log house by felling trees and putting them one upon another, then the fortune belongs to Mr Rockefeller in the same way as the log house belongs to the pioneer. And if the social inferences that are drawn from the theory of natural liberty and natural value are correct, the millionaire and the landlord, the plutocrat and the pioneer, the wage earner and the capitalist, have each all the right to do what he will with his own. For every man in this just world gets what is coming to him. He gets what he is worth, and he is worth what he gets.

But if one knocks out the keystone of the arch in the form of a proposition that natural value conforms to the cost of production, then the whole edifice collapses and must be set up again, upon another plan and on another foundation, stone by stone.

4 Work and wages

WAGES AND PRICES, then, if the argument recited in the preceding chapter of this series holds good, do not under free competition tend towards social justice. It is not true that every man gets
what he produces. It is not true that enormous salaries represent
enormous productive services and that humble wages correspond to
a humble contribution to the welfare of society. Prices, wages,
salaries, interest, rent and profits do not, if left to themselves, follow
the simple law of natural justice. To think so is an idle dream, the
dream of the quietist who may slumber too long and be roused to a
rude awakening or perish, perhaps, in his sleep. His dream is not so
dangerous as the contrasted dream of the socialist, now threatening
to walk abroad in his sleep, but both in their degree are dreams and
nothing more.

The real truth is that prices and wages are all the various payments from hand to hand in industrial society, are the outcome of a
complex of competing forces that are not based upon justice but
upon 'economic strength.' To elucidate this it is necessary to plunge
into the jungle of pure economic theory. The way is arduous. There
are no flowers upon the path. And out of this thicket, alas, no two
people ever emerge hand in hand in concord. Yet it is a path that
must be traversed. Let us take, then, as a beginning the very simplest
case of the making of a price. It is the one which is sometimes called
in books on economics the case of an unique monopoly. Suppose
that I offer for sale the manuscript of the Pickwick Papers, or
Shakespere's skull, or, for the matter of that, the skull of John
Smith, what is the sum that I shall receive for it? It is the utmost
that any one is willing to give for it. That is all one can say about it.
There is no question here of cost or what I paid for the article or of
anything else except the amount of the willingness to pay on the
part of the highest bidder. It would be possible, indeed, for a bidder
to take the article from me by force. But this we presume to be
prevented by the law, and for this reason we referred above not to
the physical strength, but to the 'economic strength' of the parties
to a bargain. By this is meant the relation that arises out of the
condition of the supply and the demand, the willingness or eagerness, or the sheer necessity, of the buyers and the sellers. People may
offer much because the thing to be acquired is an absolute necessity
without which they perish; a drowning man would sell all that he
had for a life belt. Or they may offer much through the sheer

abundance of their other possessions. A millionaire might offer more for a life belt as a souvenir than a drowning man could pay for it to save his life.

Yet out of any particular conjunction between desires on the one hand and goods or services on the other arises a particular equation of demand and supply, represented by a particular price. All of this, of course, is ABC, and I am not aware that anybody doubts it.

Now let us make the example a little more elaborate. Suppose that one single person owned all the food supply of a community isolated from the outside world. The price which he could exact would be the full measure of all the possessions of his neighbours up to the point at least where they would commit suicide rather than pay. True, in such a case as this, 'economic strength' would probably be broken down by the intrusion of physical violence. But in so far as it held good the price of food would be based upon it.

Prices such as are indicated here were dismissed by the earlier economist as mere economic curiosities. John Stuart Mill has something to say about the price of a 'music box in the wilds of Lake Superior,' which, as he perceived, would not be connected with the expense of producing it, but might be vastly more or perhaps decidedly less. But Mill might have said the same thing about the price of a music box, provided it was properly patented, anywhere at all. For the music box and Shakespere's skull and the corner in wheat are all merely different kinds of examples of the things called a monopoly sale.

Now let us change the example a little further. Suppose that the monopolist has for sale not simply a fixed and definite quantity of a certain article, but something which he can produce in larger quantities as desired. At what price will he now sell? If he offers the article at a very high price only a few people will take it: if he lowers the price there will be more and more purchasers. His interest seems divided. He will want to put the price as high as possible so that the profit on each single article (over what it costs him to produce it) will be as great as possible. But he will also want to make as many sales as he possibly can, which will induce him to set the price low enough to bring in new buyers. But, of course, if he puts the price so low that it only covers the cost of making the goods his profit is all gone and the mere multiplicity of sales is no good to him. He must try therefore to find a point of maximum profit where, having in view both the number of sales and the profit over cost on each sale the net profit is at its greatest. This gives us the fundamental law of monopoly price. It is to be noted that under modern conditions of production the cost of manufacture per article decreases to a great extent in proportion as a larger and larger number is produced and thus the widening of the sale lowers the proportionate cost. In any particular case, therefore, it may turn out that the price that suits the monopolist's own interest is quite a low price, one such as to allow for an enormous quantity of sales and a very low cost of manufacture. This, we say, *may* be the case. But it is not so of necessity. In and of itself the monopoly price corresponds to the monopolist's profit and not to cheapness of sale. The price *may* be set far above the cost.

And now notice the peculiar relation that is set up between the monopolist's production and the satisfaction of human wants. In proportion as the quantity produced is increased the lower must the price be set in order to sell the whole output. If the monopolist insisted on turning out more and more of his goods, the price that people would give would fall until it barely covered the cost, then till it was less than cost, then to a mere fraction of the cost and finally to nothing at all. In other words, if one produces a large enough quantity of anything it becomes worthless. It loses all its value just as soon as there is enough of it to satisfy, and over-satisfy the wants of humanity. Thus if the world produces three and a half billion bushels of wheat it can be sold, let us say, at two dollars a bushel; but if it produced twice as much it might well be found that it would only sell for fifty cents a bushel. The value of the bigger supply as a total would actually be less than that of the smaller. And if the supply were big enough it would be worth, in the economic sense, just nothing at all. This peculiarity is spoken of in economic theory as the paradox of value. It is referred to in the older books either as an economic curiosity or as a mere illustration in extreme terms of the relation of supply to price. Thus in many books the story is related of how the East India Companies used at times deliberately to destroy a large quantity of tea in order that by selling a lesser amount they might reap a larger profit than by selling a greater.

But in reality this paradox of value is the most fundamental proposition in economic science. Precisely here is found the key to the operation of the economic society in which we live. The world's production is aimed at producing 'values,' not in producing plenty. If by some mad access of misdirected industry we produced enough and too much of everything, our whole machinery of buying and selling would break down. This indeed does happen constantly on a small scale in the familiar phenomenon of over-production. But in the organization in which we live over-production tends to check itself at once. If the world's machinery threatens to produce a too great plenty of any particular thing, then it turns itself towards producing something else of which there is not yet enough. This is done quite unconsciously without any philanthropic intent on the part of the individual producer and without any general direction in the way of a social command. The machine does it of itself. When there is *enough* the wheels slacken and stop. This sounds at first hearing most admirable. But let it be noted that the *'enough'* here in question does not mean enough to satisfy human wants. In fact it means precisely the converse. It means enough *not* to satisfy them, and to leave the selling price of the things made at the point of profit.

Let it be observed also that we have hitherto been speaking as if all things were produced under a monopoly. The objection might at once be raised that with competitive producers the price will also keep falling down towards cost and will not be based upon the point of maximum profit. We shall turn to this objection in a moment. But one or two other points must be considered before doing so.

In the first place in following out such an argument as the present in regard to the peculiar shortcomings of the system under which we live, it is necessary again and again to warn the reader against a hasty conclusion to the possibilities of altering and amending it. The socialist reads such criticism as the above with impatient approval. 'Very well,' he says, 'the whole organization is wrong and works badly. Now let us abolish it altogether and make a better one.' But in doing so he begs the whole question at issue. The point is, *can* we make a better one or must we be content with patching up the old one? Take an illustration. Scientists tell us that from the point of view of optics the human eye is a clumsy instrument poorly con- trived for its work. A certain great authority once said that if he had made it he would have been ashamed of it. This may be true. But the eye unfortunately is all we have to see by. If we destroy our eyes in the hope of making better ones we may go blind. The best that we can do is to improve our sight by adding a pair of spectacles. So it is with the organization of society. Faulty though it is, it does the work after a certain fashion. We may apply to it with advantage the spectacles of social reform, but what the socialist offers us is total blindness. But of this presently.

To return to the argument. Let us consider next what wages the monopolist in the cases described above will have to pay. We take for granted that he will only pay as much as he has to. How much will this be? Clearly enough it will depend altogether on the number of available working men capable of doing the work in question and the situation in which they find themselves. It is again a case of relative 'economic strength.' The situation may be altogether in favour of the employer or altogether in favour of the men, or may occupy a middle ground. If the men are so numerous that there are more of them than are needed for the work, and if there is no other occupation for them they must accept a starvation wage. If they are so few in number that they can *all* be employed, and if they are so well organized as to act together, they can in their turn exact any wage up to the point that leaves no profit for the employer himself at all. Indeed for a short time wages might even pass this point, the monopolist employer being willing (for various reasons, all quite obvious) actually to pay more as wages than he gets as return and to carry on business at a loss for the sake of carrying it on at all. Clearly, then, wages, as Adam Smith said, 'are the result of a dispute' in which either party must be pushed to the wall. The employer may have to pay so much that there is nothing or practically nothing left for himself, or so little that his workmen can just exist and no more. These are the upward and downward limits of the wages in the cases described.

It is therefore obvious that if all the industries in the world were carried on as a series of separate monopolies, there would be exactly the kind of rivalry or competition of forces represented by the consumer insisting on paying as little as possible, the producer charging the most profitable price and paying the lowest wage that he could, and the wage earner demanding the highest wage that he could get. The equilibrium would be an unstable one. It would be constantly displaced and shifted by the movement of all sorts of social forces — by changes of fashion, by abundance or scarcity of crops, by alterations in the technique of industry and by the cohesion or the slackening of the organization of any group of workers. But the balanced forces once displaced would be seen constantly to come to an equilibrium at a new point.

All this has been said of industry under monopoly. But it will be seen to apply in its essentials to what we call competitive industry. Here indeed certain new features come in. Not one employer but many produce each kind of article. And, as far as each employer can see by looking at his own horizon, what he does is merely to produce as much as he can sell at a price that pays him. Since all the other employers are doing this, there will be, under competition, a constant tendency to cut the prices down to the lowest that is consistent with what the employer has to pay as wages and interest. This point, which was called by the orthodox economists the 'cost,' is not in any true and fundamental sense of the words the 'cost' at all. It is merely a limit represented by what the other parties to the bargain are able to exact. The whole situation is in a condition of unstable equilibrium in which the conflicting forces represented by the interests of the various parties pull in different directions. The employers in any one line of industry and all their wage earners and salaried assistants have one and the same interest as against the consumer. They want the selling price to be as high as possible. But the employers are against one another as wanting, each of them, to make as many sales as possible, and each and all the employers are against the wage earners in wanting to pay as low wages as possible. If all the employers unite, the situation turns to a monopoly, and the price paid by the consumer is settled on the monopoly basis already described. The employers can then dispute it out with their working men as to how much wages shall be. If the employers are not united, then at each and every moment they are in conflict both with the consumer and with their wage earners. Thus the whole scene of industry represents a vast and unending conflict, a fermentation in which the moving bubbles crowd for space, expanding and breaking one against the other. There is no point of rest. There is no real fixed 'cost' acting as a basis. Anything that any one person or group of persons – worker or master, landlord or capitalist – is able to exact owing to the existing conditions of demand or supply, becomes a 'cost' from the point of view of all the others. There is nothing in this 'cost' which proportions to it the quantity of labour, or of time, or of skill or of any other measure physical or psychological of the effort involved. And there is nothing whatever in it which proportions to it social justice. It is the war of each against all. Its only mitigation is that it is carried on under the set of rules represented by the state and the law.

The tendencies involved may be best illustrated by taking one or two extreme or exaggerated examples, not meant as facts but only to make clear the nature of social and industrial forces among which we live.

What, for example, will be the absolute maximum to which wages in general could be forced? Conceivably and in the purest and thinnest of theory, they could include the whole product of the labour of society with just such a small fraction left over for the employers, the owners of capital and the owners of land to induce them to continue acting as part of the machine. That is to say, if all the labourers all over the world, to the last one, were united under a single control they could force the other economic classes of society to something approaching a starvation living. In practice this is nonsense. In theory it is an excellent starting point for thought.

And how short could the hours of the universal united workers be made? As short as ever they liked: an hour a day: ten minutes, anything they like; but of course with the proviso that the shorter the hours the less the total of things produced to be divided. It is true that up to a certain point shortening the hours of labour actually increases the total product. A ten-hour day, speaking in general terms and leaving out individual exceptions, is probably more productive than a day of twelve. It may very well be that an eight-hour day will prove, presently if not immediately, to be more productive than one of ten. But somewhere the limit is reached and gross production falls. The supply of things in general gets shorter. But note that this itself would not matter much, if somehow and in some way not yet found, the shortening of the production of goods cut out the luxuries and superfluities first. Mankind at large might well trade leisure for luxuries. The shortening of hours with the corresponding changes in the direction of production is really the central problem in social reform. I propose to return to it in the concluding chapter of these papers, but for the present it is only noted in connection with the general scheme of industrial relations.

Now let us ask to what extent any particular section or part of industrial society can succeed in forcing up wages or prices as against the others. In pure theory they may do this almost to any extent, provided that the thing concerned is a necessity and is without a substitute and provided that their organization is complete and unbreakable. If all the people concerned in producing coal, masters and men, owners of mines and operators of machinery, could stand out for their price, there is no limit, short of putting all the rest of the world on starvation rations, to what they might get. In practice and in reality a thousand things intervene — the impossibility of such complete unity, the organization of the other parties, the existing of national divisions among industrial society, sentiment, decency, fear. The proposition is only 'pure theory.' But its use as such is to dispose of any such idea as that there is a natural price of coal or of anything else.

The above is true of any article of necessity. It is true though in a less degree of things of luxury. If all the makers of instruments of music, masters and men, capitalists and workers, were banded together in a tight and unbreakable union, then the other economic classes must either face the horrors of a world without pianolas and trombones, or hand over the price demanded. And what is true of coal and music is true all through the whole mechanism of industry.

Or take the supreme case of the owners of land. If all of them acted together, with their legal rights added into one, they could order the rest of the world either to get off it or to work at starvation wages.

Industrial society is therefore mobile, elastic, standing at any moment in a temporary and unstable equilibrium. But at any particular moment the possibility of a huge and catastrophic shift such as those described is out of the question except at the price of a general collapse. Even a minor dislocation breaks down a certain part of the machinery of society. Particular groups of workers are thrown out of place. There is no other place where they can fit in, or at any rate not immediately. The machine labours heavily. Ominous mutterings are heard. The legal framework of the State and of obedience to the law in which industrial society is set threatens to break asunder. The attempt at social change threatens a social revolution in which the whole elaborate mechanism would burst into fragments.

In any social movement, then, change and alteration in a new direction must be balanced against the demands of social stability. Some things are possible and some are not; some are impossible to-day, and possible or easy tomorrow. Others are forever out of the question.

But this much at least ought to appear clear if the line of argument indicated above is accepted, namely, that there is no great hope for universal betterment of society by the mere advance of technical industrial progress and by the unaided play of the motive of every man for himself.

The enormous increase in the productivity of industrial effort would never of itself have elevated by one inch the lot of the working class. The rise of wages in the nineteenth century and the shortening of hours that went with it was due neither to the advance in mechanical power nor to the advance in diligence and industriousness, nor to the advance, if there was any, in general kindliness. It was due to the organization of labour. Mechanical progress makes higher wages possible. It does not, of itself, advance them by a single farthing. Labour-saving machinery does not of itself save the working world a single hour of toil: it only shifts it from one task to another.

Against a system of unrestrained individualism, energy, industriousness and honesty might shatter itself in vain. The thing is merely a race in which only one can be first no matter how great the speed of all; a struggle in which one, and not all, can stand upon the shoulders of the others. It is the restriction of individualism by the force of organization and by legislation that has brought to the world whatever social advance has been achieved by the great mass of the people.

The present moment is in a sense the wrong time to say this. We no longer live in an age when down-trodden labourers meet by candlelight with the ban of the law upon their meeting. These are the days when 'labour' is triumphant, and when it ever threatens in the overweening strength of its own power to break industrial society in pieces in the fierce attempt to do in a day what can only be done in a generation. But truth is truth. And anyone who writes of the history of the progress of industrial society owes it to the truth to acknowledge the vast social achievement of organized labour in the past.

And what of the future?

By what means and in what stages can social progress be further accelerated? This I propose to treat in the succeeding chapters, dealing first with the proposals of the socialists and the revolutionaries, and finally with the prospect for a sane, orderly and continuous social reform.

5 The land of dreams: the Utopia of the socialist

WHO IS THERE that has not turned at times from the fever and fret of the world we live in, from the spectacle of its wasted energy, its wild frenzy of work and its bitter inequality, to the land of dreams, to the pictured vision of the world as it might be?

Such a vision has haunted in all ages the brooding mind of mankind; and every age has fashioned for itself the image of a 'somewhere' or 'nowhere' – a Utopia in which there should be equality and justice for all. The vision itself is an outcome of that divine discontent which raises man above his environment.

Every age has had its socialism, its communism, its dream of bread and work for all. But the dream has varied always in the likeness of the thought of the time. In earlier days the dream was not one of social wealth. It was rather a vision of the abnegation of riches, of humble possessions shared in common after the manner of the unrealized ideal of the Christian faith. It remained for the age of machinery and power to bring forth another and a vastly more potent socialism. This was no longer a plan whereby all might be poor together, but a proposal that all should be rich together. The collectivist state advocated by the socialist of to-day has scarcely anything in common with the communism of the middle ages.

Modern socialism is the direct outcome of the age of machine production. It takes its first inspiration from glaring contrasts between riches and poverty presented by the modern era, from the strange paradox that has been described above between human power and its failure to satisfy human want. The nineteenth century brought with it the factory and the factory slavery of the Lancashire children, the modern city and city slum, the plutocracy and the proletariat, and all the strange discrepancy between wealth and want that has disfigured the material progress of the last hundred years. The rising splendour of capitalism concealed from the dazzled eye the melancholy spectacle of the new industrial poverty that lay in the shadow behind it.

The years that followed the close of the Napoleonic wars in 1815 were in many senses years of unexampled misery. The accumulated burden of the war lay heavy upon Europe. The rise of the new machine power had dislocated the older system. A multitude of landless men clamored for bread and work. Pauperism spread like a plague. Each new invention threw thousands of hand-workers out of employment. The law still branded as conspiracy any united attempt of workingmen to raise wages or to shorten the hours of work. At the very moment when the coming of steam power and the use of modern machinery were piling up industrial fortunes undreamed of before, destitution, pauperism and unemployment seemed more widespread and more ominous than ever. In this rank atmosphere germinated modern socialism. The writings of Marx and Engels and Louis Blanc were inspired by what they saw about them.

From its very cradle socialism showed the double aspect which has distinguished it ever since. To the minds of some it was the faith of the insurrectionist, something to be achieved by force; 'bourgeois' society must be overthrown by force of arms; if open and fair fighting was not possible against such great odds, it must be blown sky-high with gunpowder. Dynamite, by the good fortune of invention, came to the revolutionary at the very moment when it was most wanted. To the men of violence, socialism was the twin brother of anarchism, born at the same time, advocating the same means and differing only as to the final end.

But to others, socialism was from the beginning, as it is to-day, a creed of peace. It advocated the betterment of society not by violence but by persuasion, by peaceful argument and the recognized rule of the majority. It is true that the earlier socialists almost to a man included, in the first passion of their denunciation, things not necessarily within the compass of purely economic reform. As children of misery they cried out against all human institutions. The bond of marriage seemed an accursed thing, the mere slavery of women. The family – the one institution in which the better side of human nature shines with an undimmed light – was to them but an engine of class oppression; the Christian churches merely the parasitic servants of the tyrannous power of a plutocratic state. The whole history of human civilization was denounced as an unredeemed record of the spoliation of the weak by the strong. Even the domain of the philosopher was needlessly invaded and all forms of speculative belief were rudely thrown aside in favour of a wooden materialism as dogmatic as any of the creeds or theories which it proposed to replace.

Thus seen, socialism appeared as the very antithesis of law and order, of love and chastity, and of religion itself. It was a tainted creed. There was blood upon its hands and bloody menace in its thoughts. It was a thing to be stamped out, to be torn up by the roots. The very soil in which it grew must be burned out with the flame of avenging justice.

Such it still appears to many people to-day. The unspeakable savagery of bolshevism has made good the wildest threats of the partisans of violence and fulfilled the sternest warnings of the conservative. To-day more than ever socialism is in danger of becoming a prescribed creed, its very name under the ban of the law, its literature burned by the hangman and a gag placed upon its mouth.

But this is neither right nor wise. Socialism, like every other impassioned human effort, will flourish best under martyrdom. It will languish and perish in the dry sunlight of open discussion.

For it must always be remembered in fairness that the creed of violence has no necessary connection with socialism. In its essential nature socialism is nothing but a proposal for certain kinds of economic reform. A man has just as much right to declare himself a socialist as he has to call himself a Seventh Day Adventist or a Prohibitionist, or a Perpetual Motionist. It is, or should be, open to him to convert others to his way of thinking. It is only time to restrain him when he proposes to convert others by means of a shotgun or by dynamite, and by forcible interference with their own rights. When he does this he ceases to be a socialist pure and simple and becomes a criminal as well. The law can deal with him as such.

But with socialism itself the law, in a free country, should have no kind of quarrel. For in the whole program of peaceful socialism there is nothing wrong at all except one thing. Apart from this it is a high and ennobling ideal truly fitted for a community of saints. And the one thing that is wrong with socialism is that it won't work. That is all. It is, as it were, a beautiful machine of which the wheels, dependent upon some unknown and uninvented motive power, refuse to turn. The unknown motive force in this case means a power of altruism, of unselfishness, of willingness to labour for the good of others, such as the human race has never known, nor is ever likely to know. But the worst public policy to pursue in reference to such a machine is to lock it up, to prohibit all examination of it and to allow it to become a hidden mystery, the whispered hope of its martyred advocates. Better far to stand it out into the open daylight, to let all who will inspect it, and to prove even to the simplest that such a contrivance once and for all and for ever cannot be made to run.

Let us turn to examine the machine.

We may omit here all discussion of the historical progress of socialism and the stages whereby it changed from the creed of a few theorists and revolutionists to being the accepted platform of great political parties, counting its adherents by the million. All of this belongs elsewhere. It suffices here to note that in the process of its rise it has chafed away much of the superfluous growth that clung to it and has become a purely economic doctrine. There is no longer any need to discuss in connection with it the justification of marriage and the family, and the rightness or wrongness of Christianity: no need to decide whether the materialistic theory of history is true or false, since nine socialists out of ten to-day have forgotten, or have never heard, what the materialistic theory of history is: no need to examine whether human history is, or is not, a mere record of class exploitation, since the controversy has long shifted to other grounds. The essential thing to-day is not the past, but the future. The question is, what does the socialist have to say about the conditions under which we live and the means that he advocates for the betterment of them?

His case stands thus. He begins his discussion with an indictment of the manifold weaknesses and the obvious injustices of the system under which we live. And in this the socialist is very largely right. He shows that under free individual competition there is a perpetual waste of energy. Competing rivals cover the same field. Even the simplest services are performed with an almost ludicrous waste of energy. In every modern city the milk supply is distributed by erratic milkmen who skip from door to door and from street to street, covering the same ground, each leaving his cans of milk here and there in a sporadic fashion as haphazard as a bee among the flowers. Contrast, says the socialist, the wasted labours of the milkman with the orderly and systematic performance of the postman, himself a little fragment of socialism. And the milkman, they tell us, is typical of modern industrial society. Competing railways run trains on parallel tracks, with empty cars that might be filled and with vast executive organizations which do ten times over the work that might be done by one. Competing stores needlessly occupy the time of hundreds of thousands of employees in a mixture of idleness and industry. An inconceivable quantity of human effort is spent on advertising, mere shouting and display, as unproductive in the social sense as the beating of a drum. Competition breaks into a dozen inefficient parts the process that might conceivably be carried out, with an infinite saving of effort, by a single guiding hand.

The socialist looking thus at the world we live in sees in it nothing but waste and selfishness and inefficiency. He looks so long that a mist comes before his eyes. He loses sight of the supreme fact that after all, in its own poor, clumsy fashion, the machine does work. He loses sight of the possibility of our falling into social chaos. He sees no longer the brink of the abyss beside which the path of progress picks its painful way. He leaps with a shout of exultation over the cliff.

And he lands, at least in imagination, in his ideal state, his Utopia. Here the noise and clamor of competitive industry is stilled. We look about us at a peaceful landscape where men and women brightly clothed and abundantly fed and warmed, sing at their easy task. There is enough for all and more than enough. Poverty has vanished. Want is unknown. The children play among the flowers. The youths and maidens are at school. There are no figures here bent with premature toil, no faces dulled and furrowed with a life of hardship. The light of education and culture has shone full on every face and illuminated it into all that it might be. The cheerful hours of easy labour vary but do not destroy the pursuit of pleasure and of recreation. Youth in such a Utopia is a very springtime of hope: adult life a busy and cheery activity: and age itself, watching from its shady bench beneath a spreading tree the labours of its children, is but a gentle retrospect from which material care has passed away.

It is a picture beautiful as the opalescent colours of a soap bubble. It is the vision of a garden of Eden from which the demon has been banished. And the Demon in question is the Private Ownership of the Means of Production. His name is less romantic than those of the wonted demons of legend and folklore. But it is at least suitable for the matter-of-fact age of machinery which he is supposed to haunt and on which he casts his evil spell. Let him be once exorcised and the ills of humanity are gone. And the exorcism, it appears, is of the simplest. Let this demon once feel the contact of state ownership of the means of production and his baneful influence will vanish into thin air as his mediaeval predecessors did at the touch of a thimbleful of holy water.

This, then, is the socialist's programme. Let 'the state' take over all the means of production — all the farms, the mines, the factories, the workshops, the ships, the railroads. Let it direct the workers towards their task in accordance with the needs of society. Let each labour for all in the measure of his strength and talent. Let each receive from all in the measure of his proper needs. No work is to be wasted: nothing is to be done twice that need only be done once. All must work and none must be idle: but the amount of work needed under these conditions will be so small, the hours so short, and the effort so slight, that work itself will no longer be the grinding monotonous toil that we know to-day, but a congenial activity pleasant in itself.

A thousand times this picture has been presented. The visionary with uplifted eyes, his gaze bent on the bright colours of the floating bubble, has voiced it from a thousand platforms. The earnest youth grinding at the academic mill has dreamed it in the pauses of his studious labour. The impassioned pedant has written it in heavy prose smothering its brightness in the dull web of his own thought. The brilliant imaginative mind has woven it into romance, making its colours brighter still with the sunlight of inspired phantasy.

But never, I think, has the picture of socialism at work been so ably and so dexterously presented as in a book that begins to be forgotten now, but which some thirty years ago took the continent by storm. This was the volume in which Mr Edward Bellamy 'looked backward' from his supposed point of vantage in the year 2000 AD and saw us as we are and as we shall be. No two plans of a socialist state are ever quite alike. But the scheme of society outlined in *Looking Backward* may be examined as the most attractive and the most consistent outline of a socialist state that has, within the knowledge of the present writer, ever been put forward. It is worth while, in the succeeding chapter to examine it in detail. No better starting point for the criticism of collectivist theories can be found than in a view of the basis on which is supposed to rest the halcyon life of Mr Bellamy's charming commonwealth.

6 How Mr Bellamy looked backwards

THE READING public is as wayward and as fickle as a bee among the flowers. It will not long pause anywhere, and it easily leaves each blossom for a better. But like the bee, while impelled by an instinct that makes it search for sugar, it sucks in therewith its solid sustenance.

I am not quite certain that the bee does exactly do this; but it is just the kind of thing that the bee is likely to do. And in any case it is precisely the thing which the reading public does. It will not read unless it is tempted by the sugary sweetness of the romantic interest. It must have its hero and its heroine and its course of love that never will run smooth. For information the reader cares nothing. If he absorbs it, it must be by accident, and unawares. He passes over the heavy tomes filled with valuable fact, and settles like the random bee upon the bright flowers of contemporary romance.

Hence if the reader is to be ensnared into absorbing something useful, it must be hidden somehow among the flowers. A treatise on religion must be disguised as a love story in which a young clergyman, sworn into holy orders, falls in love with an actress. The facts of history are imparted by a love story centering around the adventures of a hitherto unknown son of Louis the Fourteenth. And a discussion of the relations of labour and capital takes the form of a romance in which the daughter of a multi-millionaire steps voluntarily out of her Fifth Avenue home to work in a steam laundry.

Such is the recognized method by which the great unthinking public is taught to think. Slavery was not fully known till Mrs Stowe wrote *Uncle Tom's Cabin*, and the slow tyranny of the law's delay was taught to the world for ever in the pages of *Bleak House*.

So it has been with socialism. No single influence ever brought its ideas and its propaganda so forcibly and clearly before the public mind as Mr Edward Bellamy's brilliant novel, *Looking Backward*, published some thirty years ago. The task was arduous. Social and economic theory is heavy to the verge of being indigestible. There is no such thing as a gay book on political economy for reading in a hammock. Yet Mr Bellamy succeeded. His book is in cold reality nothing but a series of conversations explaining how a socialist commonwealth is supposed to work. Yet he contrives to bring into it a hero and a heroine, and somehow the warm beating of their hearts and the stolen glances in their eyes breathe into the dry dust of economic argument the breath of life. Nor was ever a better presentation made of the essential programme of socialism.

It is worth while then, as was said in the preceding chapter, to consider Mr Bellamy's commonwealth as the most typical and the most carefully constructed of all the ready-made socialisms that have been put forward.

The mere machinery of the story can be lightly passed over. It is intended simply as the sugar that lures the random bee. The hero, living in Boston in 1887, is supposed to fall asleep in a deep, underground chamber which he has made for himself as a remedy against a harassing insomnia. Unknown to the sleeper the house above his retreat is burned down. He remains in a trance for a hundred and thirteen years and awakes to find himself in the Boston of the year 2000 AD. Kind hands remove him from his sepulcher. He is revived. He finds himself under the care of a certain learned and genial Dr Leete, whose house stands on the very site where once the sleeper lived. The beautiful daughter of Dr Leete looks upon the newcomer from the lost world with eyes in which, to the mind of the sagacious reader, love is seen at once to dawn. In reality she is the great-granddaughter of the fiancée whom the sleeper was to have married in his former life; thus a faint suggestion of the transmigration of souls illuminates their intercourse. Beyond that there is no story and at the end of the book the sleeper, in another dream, is conveniently transported back to 1887 which he can now contrast, in horror, with the ideal world of 2000 AD.

And what was this world? The sleeper's first vision of it was given him by Dr. Leete, who took him to the house top and let him see the Boston of the future. Wide avenues replace the crowded, noisy streets. There are no shops but only here and there among the trees great marble buildings, the emporiums from which the goods are delivered to the purple public.

And the goods are delivered indeed! Dr Leete explains it all with intervals of grateful cigar smoking and of music and promenades with the beautiful Edith, and meals in wonderful communistic restaurants with romantic waiters, who feel themselves, *mirabile dictu,* quite independent.

And this is how the commonwealth operates. Everybody works or at least works until the age of forty, so that it may be truly said in these halcyon days everybody works but father. But the work of life does not begin till education ends at the age of twenty-one. After that all the young men and women pass for three years into the general 'Industrial Army,' much as the young men used to pass into the ranks of conscription. Afterwards each person may select any trade that he likes. But the hours are made longer or shorter according to whether too many or too few young people apply to come in. A gardener works for more hours than a scavenger. Yet all occupations are equally honourable. The wages of all the people are equal; or rather there are no wages at all, as the workers merely receive cards, which entitle them to goods of such and such a quantity at any of the emporiums. The cards are punched out as the goods are used. The goods are all valued according to the amount of time used in their making and each citizen draws out the same total amount. But he may take it out in installments just as he likes, drawing many things one month and few the next. He may even get goods in advance if he has any special need. He may, within a certain time limit, save up his cards, but it must be remembered that the one thing which no card can buy and which no citizens can own is the 'means of production.' These belong collectively to all. Land, mines, machinery, factories and the whole mechanism of transport, these things are public property managed by the state. Its workers in their use of them are all directed by public authority as to what they shall make and when they shall make it, and how much shall be made. On these terms all share alike; the cripple receives as much as the giant; the worker of exceptional dexterity and energy the same as his slower and less gifted fellow.

All the management, the control – and let this be noted, for there is no escape from it either by Mr Bellamy or by anybody else – is exercised by boards of officials elected by the people. All the complex organization by which production goes on by which the workers are supervised and shifted from trade to trade, by which their requests for a change of work or an extension of credit are heard and judged – all of this is done by the elected 'bosses.' One lays stress on this not because it is Mr Bellamy's plan, but because it is, and it *has to be,* the plan of anybody who constructs a socialist commonwealth.

Mr Bellamy has many ingenious arrangements to meet the needs of people who want to be singers or actors or writers – in other words, who do not want to work. They may sing or act as much as they like, provided that enough other people will hand over enough of their food cards to keep them going. But if no one wants to hear them sing or see them act they may starve – just as they do now. Here the author harks back unconsciously to his nineteenth century individualism; he need not have done so; other socialist writers would have it that one of the everlasting boards would 'sit on' every aspiring actor or author before he was allowed to begin. But we may take it either way. It is not the major point. There is no need to discuss the question of how to deal with the artist under socialism. If the rest of it were all right, no one need worry about the artist. Perhaps he would do better without being remunerated at all. It is doubtful whether the huge commercial premium that greets success to-day does good or harm. But let it pass. It is immaterial to the present matter.

One comes back to the essential question of the structure of the commonwealth. Can such a thing, or anything conceived in its likeness, possibly work? The answer is, and must be, absolutely and emphatically no.

Let anyone conversant with modern democracy as it is – not as its founders dreamed of it – picture to himself the operation of a system whereby anything and everything is controlled by elected officials, from whom there is no escape, outside of whom is no livelihood and to whom all men must bow! Democracy, let us grant it, is the best system of government as yet operative in this world of sin. Beside autocratic kingship it shines with a white light; it is obviously the portal of the future. But we know it now too well to idealize its merits.

A century and a half ago when the world was painfully struggling out of the tyranny of autocratic kingship, when English liberalism was in its cradle, when Thomas Jefferson was composing the immortal phrases of the Declaration of Independence and unknown patriots dreamed of freedom in France – at such an epoch it was but natural that the principle of popular election should be idealized as the sovereign remedy for the political evils of mankind. It was natural and salutary that it should be so. The force of such idealization helped to carry forward the human race to a new milestone on the path of progress.

But when it is proposed to entrust to the method of elective control not a part but the whole of the fortunes of humanity, to commit to it not merely the form of government and the necessary maintenance of law, order and public safety, but the whole operation of the production and distribution of the world's goods, the case is altered. The time is ripe then for retrospect over the experience of the nineteenth century and for a realization of what has proved in that experience the peculiar defects of elective democracy.

Mr Bellamy pictures his elected managers – as every socialist has to do – as a sagacious and paternal group, free from the interest of self and the play of the baser passions and animated only by the thought of the public good. Gravely they deliberate; wisely and justly they decide. Their gray heads – for Bellamy prefers them old – are bowed in quiet confabulation over the nice adjustment of the national production, over the petition of this or that citizen. The public care sits heavily on their breast. Their own peculiar fortune they have lightly passed by. They do not favour their relations or their friends. They do not count their hours of toil. They do not enumerate their gain. They work, in short, as work the angels.

Now let me ask in the name of sanity where are such officials to be found? Here and there, perhaps, one sees in the world of to-day in the stern virtue of an honourable public servant some approximation to such a civic ideal. But how much, too, has been seen of the rule of 'cliques' and 'interests' and 'bosses'; of the election of genial incompetents popular as spendthrifts; of crooked partisans warm to their friends and bitter to their enemies; of administration by a party for a party; and of the insidious poison of commercial greed defiling the wells of public honesty. The unending conflict between business and politics, between the private gain and the public good, has been for two generations the despair of modern democracy. It turns this way and that in its vain effort to escape corruption. It puts its faith now in representative legislatures, and now in appointed boards and commissions; it appeals to the vote of the whole people or it places an almost autocratic power and a supreme responsibility in the hands of a single man. And nowhere has the escape been found. The melancholy lesson is being learned that the path of human progress is arduous and its forward movement slow and that no mere form of government can aid unless it is inspired by a higher public spirit of the individual citizen than we have yet managed to achieve.

And of the world of to-day, be it remembered, elective democratic control covers only a part of the field. Under socialism it covers it all. To-day in our haphazard world a man is his own master; often indeed the mastership is but a pitiful thing, little more than being master of his own failure and starvation; often indeed the dead weight of circumstance, the accident of birth, the want of education, may so press him down that his freedom is only a mockery. Let us grant all that. But under socialism freedom is gone. There is nothing but the rule of the elected boss. The worker is commanded to his task and obey he must. If he will not, there is, there can only be, the prison and the scourge, or to be cast out in the wilderness to starve.

Consider what it would mean to be under a socialist state. Here for example is a worker who is, who says he is, too ill to work. He begs that he may be set free. The grave official, as Mr Bellamy sees him, looks at the worker's tongue. 'My poor fellow,' says he, 'you are indeed ill. Go and rest yourself under a shady tree while the others are busy with the harvest.' So speaks the ideal official dealing with the ideal citizen in the dream life among the angels. But suppose that the worker, being not an angel but a human being, is but a mere hulking, lazy brute who prefers to sham sick rather than endure the tedium of toil. Or suppose that the grave official is not an angel, but a man of hateful heart or one with a personal spite to vent upon his victim. What then? How could one face a régime in which the everlasting taskmaster held control? There is nothing like it among us at the present day except within the melancholy precincts of the penitentiary. There and there only, the socialist system is in operation.

Who can deny that under such a system the man with the glib tongue and the persuasive manner, the babbling talker and the scheming organizer, would secure all the places of power and profit, while patient merit went to the wall?

Or turn from the gray officials to the purple citizens of the soap bubble commonwealth of socialism. All work, we are told, and all receive their remuneration. We must not think of it as money-wages, but, all said and done, an allotted share of goods, marked out upon a card, comes pretty much to the same thing. The wages that the citizens receive must either be equal or not equal. That at least is plain logic. Either everybody gets exactly the same wages irrespective of capability and diligence, or else the wages or salaries or whatever one calls them, are graded, so that one receives much and the other little.

Now either of these alternatives spells disaster. If the wages are graded according to capacity, then the grading is done by the ever-lasting elective officials. They can, and they will, vote themselves and their friends or adherents into the good jobs and the high places. The advancement of a bright and capable young man will depend, not upon what he does, but upon what the elected bosses are pleased to do with him; not upon the strength of his own hands, but upon the strength of the 'pull' that he has with the bosses who run the part of the industry that he is in. Unequal wages under socialism would mean a fierce and corrupt scramble for power, office and emolument, beside which the utmost aberrations of Tammany Hall would seem as innocuous as a Sunday School Picnic.

'But,' objects Mr Bellamy or any other socialist, 'you forget. Please remember that under socialism the scramble for wealth is limited; no man can own capital, but only consumption goods. The most that any man may acquire is merely the articles that he wants to consume, not the engines and machinery of production itself. Hence even avarice dwindles and dies, when its wonted food of "capitalism" is withdrawn.'

But surely this point of view is the very converse of the teachings of common sense. 'Consumption goods' are the very things that we *do* want. All else is but a means to them. One admits, as per exception, the queer acquisitiveness of the miser-millionaire, playing the game for his own sake. Undoubtedly he exists. Undoubtedly his existence is a product of the system, a pathological product, a kind of elephantiasis of individualism. But speaking broadly, consumption goods, present or future, are the end in sight of the industrial struggle. Give me the houses and the gardens, the yachts, the motor cars and the champagne and I do not care who owns the gravel crusher and the steam plow. And if under a socialist commonwealth a man can vote to himself or gain by the votes of his adherents, a vast income of consumption goods and leave to his unhappy fellow a narrow minimum of subsistence, then the resulting evil of inequality is worse, far worse than it could even be to-day.

Or try, if one will, the other horn of the dilemma. That, too, one will find as ill a resting place as an upright thistle. Let the wages – as with Mr Bellamy – all be equal. The managers then cannot vote themselves large emoluments if they try. But what about the purple citizens? Will they work, or will they lie round in their purple garments and loaf? Work? Why should they work, their pay is there 'fresh and fresh'? Why should they turn up on time for their task? Why should they not dawdle at their labour sitting upon the fence in endless colloquy while the harvest rots upon the stalk? If among them is one who cares to work with a fever of industry that even socialism cannot calm, let him do it. We, his fellows, will take our time. Our pay is there as certain and as sound as his. Not for us the eager industry and the fond plans for the future – for the home and competence – that spurred on the strenuous youth of old days – not for us the earnest planning of the husband and wife thoughtful and anxious for the future of their little ones. Not for us the honest penny saved for a rainy day. Here in the dreamland of socialism there are no rainy days. It is sunshine all the time in this lotus land of the loafer. And for the future, let the 'state' provide; for the children's welfare let the 'state' take thought; while we live it shall feed us, when we fall ill it shall tend us and when we die it shall bury us. Meantime let us eat, drink and be merry and work as little as we may. Let us sit among the flowers. It is too hot to labour. Let us warm ourselves beside the public stove. It is too cold to work.

But what? Such conduct, you say, will not be allowed in the commonwealth. Idleness and slovenly, careless work will be forbidden? Ah! then you must mean that beside the worker will be the overseer with the whip; the timeclock will mark his energy upon its dial; the machine will register his effort; and if he will not work there is lurking for him in the background the shadowed door of the prison. Exactly and logically so. Socialism, in other words, is slavery.

But here the socialist and his school interpose at once with an objection. Under the socialist commonwealth, they say, the people will want to work; they will have acquired a new civic spirit; they will work eagerly and cheerfully for the sake of the public good and from their love of the system under which they live. The loafer will be extinct. The sponge and the parasite will have perished. Even crime itself, so the socialist tells us, will diminish to the vanishing point, till there is nothing of it except here and there a sort of pathological survival, an atavism, or a 'throwing back' to the forgotten sins of the grandfathers. Here and there, some poor fellow afflicted with this disease may break into my socialistic house and steal my pictures and my wine. Poor chap! Deal with him very gently. He is not wicked. He is ill.

This last argument, in a word, begs the whole question. With perfect citizens any government is good. In a population of angels a socialistic commonwealth would work to perfection. But until we have the angels we must keep the commonwealth waiting.

Nor is it necessary here to discuss the hundred and one modifications of the socialistic plan. Each and all fail for one and the same reason. The municipal socialist, despairing of the huge collective state, dreams of his little town as an organic unit in which all share alike; the syndicalist in his fancy sees his trade united into a co-operative body in which all are equal; the gradualist, in whose mind lingers the leaven of doubt, frames for himself a hazy vision of a prolonged preparation for the future, of socialism achieved little by little, the citizens being trained as it goes on till they are to reach somehow or somewhere in cloud land the nirvana of the elimination of self; like indeed, they are, to the horse in the ancient fable that was being trained to live without food but died, alas, just as the experiment was succeeding.

There is no way out. Socialism is but a dream, a bubble floating in the air. In the light of its opalescent colours we may see many visions of what we might be if we were better than we are, we may learn much that is useful as to what we can be even as we are; but if we mistake the floating bubble for the marble palaces of the city of desire, it will lead us forward in our pursuit till we fall over the edge of the abyss beyond which is chaos.

7 What is possible and what is not

SOCIALISM, THEN, will not work, and neither will individualism, or at least the older individualism that we have hitherto made the basis of the social order. Here, therefore, stands humanity, in the middle of its narrow path in sheer perplexity, not knowing which way to turn. On either side is the brink of an abyss. On one hand is the yawning gulf of social catastrophe represented by socialism. On the other, the slower, but no less inevitable disaster that would attend the continuation in its present form of the system under which we have lived. Either way lies destruction; the one swift and immediate as a fall from a great height; the other gradual, but equally dreadful, as the slow strangulation in a morass. Somewhere between the two lies such narrow safety as may be found.

The Ancients were fond of the metaphor, taken from the vexed Sicilian Seas, of Scylla and Charybdis. The twin whirlpools threatened the affrighted mariner on either side. To avoid one he too hastily cast the ship to destruction in the other. Such is precisely the position that has been reached at the present crisis in the course of human progress. When we view the shortcomings of the present individualism, its waste of energy, its fretful overwork, its cruel inequality and the bitter lot that it brings to the uncounted millions of the submerged, we are inclined to cry out against it, and to listen with a ready ear to the easy promises of the idealist. But when we turn to the contrasted fallacies of socialism, its obvious impracticality and the dark gulf of social chaos that yawns behind it, we are driven back shuddering to cherish rather the ills we have than fly to others we know not of.

Yet out of the whole discussion of the matter some few things begin to merge into the clearness of certain day. It is clear enough on the one hand that we can expect no sudden and complete transformation of the world in which we live. Such a process is impossible. The industrial system is too complex, its roots are too deeply struck and its whole organism of too delicate a growth to permit us to tear it from the soil. Nor is humanity itself fitted for the kind of transformation which fills the dreams of the perfectionist. The principle of selfishness that has been the survival instinct of existence since life first crawled from the slime of a world in evolution, is as yet but little mitigated. In the long process of time some higher cosmic sense may take its place. It has not done so yet.

If the kingdom of socialism were opened tomorrow, there are but
few fitted to enter.

But on the other hand it is equally clear that the doctrine of
'every man for himself,' as it used to be applied, is done with forever. The time has gone by when a man shall starve asking in vain for
work; when the listless outcast shall draw his rags shivering about
him unheeded of his fellows; when children shall be born in hunger
and bred in want and broken in toil with never a chance in life. If
nothing else will end these things, fear will do it. The hardest capitalist that ever gripped his property with the iron clasp of legal right
relaxes his grasp a little when he thinks of the possibilities of a social
conflagration. In this respect five years of war have taught us more
than a century of peace. It has set in a clear light new forms of social
obligation. The war brought with it conscription – not as we used to
see it, as the last horror of military tyranny, but as the crowning
pride of democracy. An inconceivable revolution in the thought of
the English speaking peoples has taken place in respect to it. The
obligation of every man, according to his age and circumstance, to
take up arms for his country and, if need be, to die for it, is henceforth the recognized basis of progressive democracy.

But conscription has its other side. The obligation to die must
carry with it the right to live. If every citizen owes it to society that
he must fight for it in case of need, then society owes to every
citizen the opportunity of a livelihood. 'Unemployment,' in the case
of the willing and able becomes henceforth a social crime. Every
democratic government must henceforth take as the starting point of
its industrial policy, that there shall be no such thing as able bodied
men and women 'out of work,' looking for occupation and unable to
find it. Work must either be found or must be provided by the state
itself.

Yet it is clear that a policy of state work and state pay for all who
are otherwise unable to find occupation involves appalling difficulties. The opportunity will loom large for the prodigal waste of
money, for the undertaking of public works of no real utility and for
the subsidizing of an army of loafers. But the difficulties, great
though they are, are not insuperable. The payment for state labour
of this kind can be kept low enough to make it the last resort rather
than the ultimate ambition of the worker. Nor need the work be

useless. In new countries, especially such as Canada and the United States and Australia, the development of latent natural assets could absorb the labour of generations. There are still unredeemed empires in the west. Clearly enough a certain modicum of public honesty and integrity is essential for such a task; more, undoubtedly, than we have hitherto been able to enlist in the service of the commonwealth. But without it we perish. Social betterment must depend at every stage on the force of public spirit and public morality that inspires it.

So much for the case of those who are able and willing to work. There remain still the uncounted thousands who by accident or illness, age or infirmity, are unable to maintain themselves. For these people, under the older dispensation, there was nothing but the poorhouse, the jail or starvation by the roadside. The narrow individualism of the nineteenth century refused to recognize the social duty of supporting somebody else's grandmother. Such charity began, and ended, at home. But even with the passing of the nineteenth century an awakened sense of the collective responsibility of society towards its weaker members began to impress itself upon public policy. Old age pension laws and national insurance against illness and accident were already being built into the legislative codes of the democratic countries. The experience of the war has enormously increased this sense of social solidarity. It is clear now that our fortunes are not in our individual keeping. We stand or fall as a nation. And the nation which neglects the aged and infirm, or which leaves a family to be shipwrecked as the result of a single accident to a breadwinner, cannot survive as against a nation in which the welfare of each is regarded as contributory to the safety of all. Even the purest selfishness would dictate a policy of social insurance.

There is no need to discuss the particular way in which this policy can best be carried out. It will vary with the circumstances of each community. The action of the municipality, or of the state or province, or of the central government itself may be called into play. But in one form or another, the economic loss involved in illness and infirmity must be shifted from the shoulders of the individual to those of society at large. There was but little realization of this obligation in the nineteenth century. Only in the sensational moments of famine, flood or pestilence was a general social effort called forth. But in the clearer view of the social bond which the war has given us we can see that famine and pestilence are merely exaggerated forms of what is happening every day in our midst.

We spoke much during the war of 'man power.' We suddenly realized that after all the greatness and strength of a nation is made up of the men and women who compose it. Its money, in the narrow sense, is nothing; a set of meaningless chips and counters piled upon a banker's table ready to fall at a touch. Even before the war we had begun to talk eagerly and anxiously of the conservation of national resources, of the need of safeguarding the forests and fisheries and the mines. These are important things. But the war has shown that the most important thing of all is the conservation of men and women.

The attitude of the nineteenth century upon this point was little short of insane. The melancholy doctrine of Malthus had perverted the public mind. Because it was difficult for a poor man to bring up a family, the hasty conclusion was reached that a family ought not to be brought up. But the war has entirely inverted and corrected this point of view. The father and mother who were able to send six sturdy, native-born sons to the conflict were regarded as benefactors of the nation. But these six sturdy sons had been, some twenty years before, six 'puling infants,' viewed with gloomy disapproval by the Malthusian bachelor. If the strength of the nation lies in its men and women there is only one way to increase it. Before the war it was thought that a simpler and easier method of increase could be found in the wholesale import of Austrians, Bulgarians and Czecho-Slovaks. The newer nations boasted proudly of their immigration tables. The fallacy is apparent now. Those who really count in a nation and those who govern its destinies for good or ill are those who are born in it.

It is difficult to over-estimate the harm that has been done to public policy by this same Malthusian theory. It has opposed to every proposal of social reform an obstacle that seemed insuperable – the danger of a rapid overincrease of population that would pauperize the community. Population, it was said, tends always to press upon the heels of subsistence. If the poor are pampered, they will breed fast: the time will come when there will not be food for all and we shall perish in a common destruction. Seen in this light, infant mortality and the cruel wastage of disease were viewed with complacence. It was 'Nature's' own process at work. The 'unfit,' so

called, were being winnowed out that only the best might survive. The biological doctrine of evolution was misinterpreted and
misapplied to social policy.

But in the organic world there is no such thing as the 'fit' or the
'unfit,' in any higher or moral sense. The most hideous forms of life
may 'survive' and thrust aside the most beautiful. It is only by a
confusion of thought that the processes of organic nature which
render every foot of fertile ground the scene of unending conflict
can be used to explain away the death of children of the slums. The
whole theory of survival is only a statement of what is, not of what
ought to be. The moment that we introduce the operation of human
volition and activity, that, too, becomes one of the factors of 'survival.' The dog, the cat, and the cow live by man's will, where the
wolf and the hyena have perished.

But it is time that the Malthusian doctrine – the fear of over-
population as a hindrance to social reform – was dismissed from
consideration. It is at best but a worn-out scarecrow shaking its vain
rags in the wind. Population, it is true, increases in a geometrical
ratio. The human race, if favoured by environment, can easily
double itself every twenty-five years. If it did this, the time must
come, through sheer power of multiplication, when there would not
be standing room for it on the globe. All of this is undeniable, but it
is quite wide of the mark. It is time enough to cross a bridge when
we come to it. The 'standing room' problem is still removed from us
by such uncounted generations that we need give no thought to it.
The physical resources of the globe are as yet only tapped, and not
exhausted. We have done little more than scratch the surface. Because we are crowded here and there in the ant-hills of our cities, we
dream that the world is full. Because, under our present system, we
do not raise enough food for all, we fear that the food supply is
running short. All this is pure fancy. Let any one consider in his
mind's eye the enormous untouched assets still remaining for mankind in the vast spaces filled with the tangled forests of South
America, or the exuberant fertility of equatorial Africa or the huge
plains of Canada, Australia, southern Siberia and the United States,
as yet only thinly dotted with human settlement. There is no need
to draw up an anxious balance sheet of our assets. There is still an
uncounted plenty. And every human being born upon the world
represents a power of work that, rightly directed, more than supplies

his wants. The fact that as an infant he does not maintain himself has nothing to do with the case. This was true even in the Garden of Eden.

The fundamental error of the Malthusian theory of population and poverty is to confound the difficulties of human organization with the question of physical production. Our existing poverty is purely a problem in the direction and distribution of human effort. It has no connection as yet with the question of the total available means of subsistence. Some day, in a remote future, in which under an improved social system the numbers of mankind might increase to the full power of the natural capacity of multiplication, such a question might conceivably disturb the equanimity of mankind. But it need not now. It is only one of many disasters that must sooner or later overtake mankind. The sun, so the astronomer tells us, is cooling down; the night is coming; an all-pervading cold will some day chill into rigid death the last vestige of organic life. Our poor planet will be but a silent ghost whirling on its dark path in the starlight. This ultimate disaster is, as far as our vision goes, inevitable. Yet no one concerns himself with it. So should it be with the danger of the ultimate overcrowding of the globe.

I lay stress upon this problem of the increase of population because, to my thinking, it is in this connection that the main work and the best hope of social reform can be found. The children of the race should be the very blossom of its fondest hopes. Under the present order and with the present gloomy preconceptions they have been the least of its collective cares. Yet here – and here more than anywhere – is the point towards which social effort and social legislation may be directed immediately and successfully. The moment that we get away from the idea that the child is a mere appendage of the parent, bound to share good fortune and ill, wealth and starvation, according to the parent's lot, the moment we regard the child as itself a member of society – clothed in social rights – a burden for the moment but an asset for the future – we turn over a new leaf in the book of human development, we pass a new milestone on the upward path of progress.

It should be recognized in the coming order of society, that every child of the nation has the right to be clothed and fed and trained irrespective of its parents' lot. Our feeble beginnings in the direction of housing, sanitation, child welfare and education, should be expanded at whatever cost into something truly national and all embracing. The ancient grudging selfishness that would not feed other people's children should be cast out. In the war time the wealthy bachelor and the spinster of advancing years took it for granted that other people's children should fight for them. The obligation must apply both ways.

No society is properly organized until every child that is born into it shall have an opportunity in life. Success in life and capacity to live we cannot give. But opportunity we can. We can at least see that the gifts that are laid in the child's cradle by nature are not obliterated by the cruel fortune of the accident of birth: that its brain and body are not stunted by lack of food and air and by the heavy burden of premature toil. The playtime of childhood should be held sacred by the nation.

This, as I see it, should be the first and the greatest effort of social reform. For the adult generation of to-day many things are no longer possible. The time has passed. We are, as viewed with a comprehensive eye, a damaged race. Few of us in mind or body are what we might be; and millions of us, the vast majority of industrial mankind known as the working class, are distorted beyond repair from what they might have been. In older societies this was taken for granted: the poor and the humble and the lowly reproduced from generation to generation, as they grew to adult life, the starved brains and stunted outlook of their forbears — starved and stunted only by lack of opportunity. For nature knows of no such differences in original capacity between the children of the fortunate and the unfortunate. Yet on this inequality, made by circumstance, was based the whole system of caste, the stratification of the gentle and the simple on which society rested. In the past it may have been necessary. It is not so now. If, with all our vast apparatus of machinery and power, we cannot so arrange society that each child has an opportunity in life, it would be better to break the machinery in pieces and return to the woods from which we came.

Put into the plainest of prose, then, we are saying that the government of every country ought to supply work and pay for the unemployed, maintenance for the infirm and aged, and education and opportunity for the children. These are vast tasks. And they involve, of course, a financial burden not dreamed of before the war. But here again the war has taught us many things. It would have seemed inconceivable before, that a man of great wealth should give one-half of his income to the state. The financial burden of the war, as the full measure of it dawned upon our minds, seemed to betoken a universal bankruptcy. But the sequel is going to show that the finance of the war will prove to be a lesson in the finance of peace. The new burden has come to stay. No modern state can hope to survive unless it meets the kind of social claims on the part of the unemployed, the destitute and the children that have been described above. And it cannot do this unless it continues to use the terrific engine of taxation already fashioned in the war. Undoubtedly the progressive income tax and the tax on profits and taxation of inheritance must be maintained to an extent never dreamed of before.

But the peace finance and the war finance will differ in one most important respect. The war finance was purely destructive. From it came national security and the triumph of right over wrong. No one would belittle the worth of the sacrifice. But in the narrower sense of production, of bread winning, there came nothing; or nothing except a new power of organization, a new technical skill and a new aspiration towards better things. But the burden of peace finance directed towards social efforts will bring a direct return. Every cent that is spent upon the betterment of the population will come back, sooner or later, as two.

But all of this deals as yet only with the field of industry and conduct in which the state rules supreme. Governmental care of the unemployed, the infant and the infirm, sounds like a chapter in socialism. If the same régime were extended over the whole area of production, we should have socialism itself and a mere soap-bubble bursting into fragments. There is no need, however, to extend the régime of compulsion over the whole field. The vast mass of human industrial effort must still lie outside of the immediate control of the government. Every man will still earn his own living and that of his family as best he can, relying first and foremost upon his own efforts.

One naturally asks, then, To what extent can social reform penetrate into the ordinary operation of industry itself? Granted that it is impossible for the state to take over the whole industry of the nation, does that mean that the present inequalities must continue? The framework in which our industrial life is set cannot be readily broken asunder. But we can to a great extent ease the rigidity of its outlines. A legislative code that starts from sounder principles than those which have obtained hitherto can do a great deal towards progressive betterment. Each decade can be an improvement upon the last. Hitherto we have been hampered at every turn by the supposed obstacle of immutable economic laws. The theory of 'natural' wages and prices of a supposed economic order that could not be disturbed, set up a sort of legislative paralysis. The first thing needed is to get away entirely from all such preconceptions, to recognize that the 'natural' order of society, based on the 'natural' liberty, does not correspond with real justice and real liberty at all, but works injustice at every turn. And at every turn intrusive social legislation must seek to prevent such injustice.

It is no part of the present essay to attempt to detail the particulars of a code of social legislation. That must depend in every case upon the particular circumstances of the community concerned. But some indication may be given here of the kind of legislation that may serve to render the conditions of industry more in conformity with social justice. Let us take, as a conspicuous example, the case of the Minimum wage law. Here is a thing sternly condemned in the older thought as an economic impossibility. It was claimed, as we have seen, that under free contract a man was paid what he earned and no law could make it more. But the older theory was wrong. The minimum wage law ought to form, in one fashion or another, a part of the code of every community. It may be applied by specific legislation from a central power, or it may be applied by the discretionary authority of district boards, or it may be regulated – as it has been in some of the beginnings already made – within the compass of each industry or trade. But the principle involved is sound. The wage as paid becomes a part of the conditions of industry. Interest, profits and, later, the direction of consumption and then of production, conform themselves to it.

True it is, that in this as in all cases of social legislation, no application of the law can be made so sweeping and so immediate as to dislocate the machine and bring industry to a stop. It is probable that at any particular time and place the legislative minimum wage cannot be very much in advance of the ordinary or average wage of the people in employment. But its virtue lies in its progression. The modest increase of to-day leads to the fuller increase of tomorrow. Properly applied, the capitalist and the employer of labour need have nothing to fear from it. Its ultimate effect will not fall upon them, but will serve merely to alter the direction of human effort.

Precisely the same reasoning holds good of the shortening of the hours of labour both by legislative enactment and by collective organization. Here again the first thing necessary is a clear vision of the goal towards which we are to strive. The hours of labour are too long. The world has been caught in the wheels of its own machinery which will not stop. With each advance in invention and mechanical power it works harder still. New and feverish desires for luxuries replace each older want as satisfied. The nerves of our industrial civilization are worn thin with the rattle of its own machinery. The industrial world is restless, over-strained and quarrelsome. It seethes with furious discontent, and looks about it eagerly for a fight. It needs a rest. It should be sent, as nerve patients are, to the seaside or the quiet of the hills. Failing this, it should at least slacken the pace of its work and shorten its working day.

And for this the thing needed is an altered public opinion on the subject of work in relation to human character and development. The nineteenth century glorified work. The poet, sitting beneath a shady tree, sang of its glories. The working man was incited to contemplate the beauty of the night's rest that followed on the exhaustion of the day. It was proved to him that if his day was dull at least his sleep was sound. The ideal of society was the cheery artisan and the honest blacksmith, awake and singing with the lark and busy all day long at the loom and the anvil, till the grateful night soothed them into well-earned slumber. This, they were told, was better than the distracted sleep of princes.

The educated world repeated to itself these grotesque fallacies till it lost sight of plain and simple truths. Seven o'clock in the morning is too early for any rational human being to be herded into a factory at the call of a steam whistle. Ten hours a day of mechanical task is too long: nine hours is too long: eight hours is too long. I am not raising here the question as to how and to what extent the eight hours can be shortened, but only urging the primary need of recognizing that a working day of eight hours is too long for the full and proper development of human capacity and for the rational enjoyment of life. There is no need to quote here to the contrary the long and sustained toil of the pioneer, the eager labour of the student, unmindful of the silent hours, or the fierce acquisitive activity of the money-maker that knows no pause. Activities such as these differ with a whole sky from the wage-work of the modern industrial worker. The task in one case is done for its own sake. It is life itself. The other is done only for the sake of the wage it brings. It is, or should be, a mere preliminary to living.

Let it be granted, of course, that a certain amount of work is an absolute necessity for human character. There is no more pathetic spectacle on our human stage than the figure of poor puppy in his beach suit and his tuxedo jacket seeking in vain to amuse himself for ever. A leisure class no sooner arises than the melancholy monotony of amusement forces it into mimic work and make-believe activities. It dare not face the empty day.

But when all is said about the horror of idleness the broad fact remains that the hours of work are too long. If we could in imagination disregard for a moment all question of how the hours of work are to be shortened and how production is to be maintained and ask only what would be the ideal number of the daily hours of compulsory work, for character's sake, few of us would put them at more than four or five. Many of us, as applied to ourselves, at least, would take a chance on character at two.

The shortening of the general hours of work, then, should be among the primary aims of social reform. There need be no fear that with shortened hours of labour the sum total of production would fall short of human needs. This, as has been shown from beginning to end of this essay, is out of the question. Human *desires* would eat up the result of ten times the work we now accomplish. Human *needs* would be satisfied with a fraction of it. But the real difficulty in the shortening of hours lies elsewhere. Here, as in the parallel case of the minimum wage, the danger is that the attempt to alter things too rapidly may dislocate the industrial machine. We ought to attempt such a shortening as will strain the machine to a breaking point, but never break it. This can be done, as with the minimum wage, partly by positive legislation and partly collective action. Not much can be done at once. But the process can be continuous. The short hours achieved with acclamation to-day will later be denounced as the long hours of to-morrow. The essential point to grasp, however, is that society at large has nothing to lose by the process. The shortened hours become a part of the framework of production. It adapts itself to it. Hitherto we have been caught in the running of our own machine: it is time that we altered the gearing of it.

The two cases selected — the minimum wage and the legislative shortening of hours — have been chosen merely as illustrations and are not exhaustive of the things that can be done in the field of possible and practical reform. It is plain enough that in many other directions the same principles may be applied. The rectification of the ownership of land so as to eliminate the haphazard gains of the speculator and the unearned increment of wealth created by the efforts of others, is an obvious case in point. The 'single taxer' sees in this a cure-all for the ills of society. But his vision is distorted. The private ownership of land is one of the greatest incentives to human effort that the world has ever known. It would be folly to abolish it, even if we could. But here as elsewhere we can seek to re-define and regulate the conditions of ownership so as to bring them more into keeping with a common sense view of social justice.

But the inordinate and fortuitous gains from land are really only one example from a general class. The war discovered the 'profiteer.' The law-makers of the world are busy now with smoking him out from his lair. But he was there all the time. Inordinate and fortuitous gain, resting on such things as monopoly, or trickery, or the mere hazards of abundance and scarcity, complying with the letter of the law but violating its spirit, are fit objects for appropriate taxation. The ways and means are difficult, but the social principle involved is clear.

We may thus form some sort of vision of the social future into which we are passing. The details are indistinct. But the outline at least in which it is framed is clear enough. The safety of the future lies in a progressive movement of social control alleviating the misery which it cannot obliterate and based upon the broad general principle of equality of opportunity. The chief immediate direction of social effort should be towards the attempt to give to every human being in childhood adequate food, clothing, education and an opportunity in life. This will prove to be the beginning of many things.